Joe Weston has a long history in the environment movement and is at present the Chairman of the Strategy Committee of Friends of the Earth UK Ltd. One of his best-known campaigns was the selling off, in tiny plots, of a small field in Oxfordshire to confuse and confound the Department of Transport's plan to build the M40 motorway across Otmoor.

Mark Levene works full time for the Peace Advertising Campaign in Oxford. He is a longstanding member of the peace movement and helped to set up the anti-Cruise missile campaign in Oxfordshire.

Frank Webster is a Senior Lecturer in Sociology at Oxford Polytechnic, the author of *The New Photography: Responsibility in Visual Communication*, Calder, 1980. He has also written extensively on computer communications technologies, including (with Kevin Robins) *Information Technology: A Luddite Analysis*, Ablex Publishing Corp, 1986.

Keith Lambe is a physicist turned sociologist. He worked for many years at the Atomic Energy Research Establishment, Harwell, and is currently a Senior Lecturer in the Department of Management and Business Studies at Oxford Polytechnic.

Michael Redclift lectures at Wye College and the Institute of Latin American Studies, University of London. He is a member of Friends of the Earth and SERA and is the author of *Development and the Environmental Crisis*, Methuen, 1984.

Jeremy Seabrook writes regularly for both the *Guardian* and *New Society* and is the author of many books. The best known of these are *What Went Wrong*, Gollancz, 1978; *Working Class Children*, Gollancz, 1982; *The Idea of Neighbourhood*, Pluto Press, 1984, and most recently *Landscapes of Poverty*, Basil Blackwell, 1985.

David Pepper is the author of *The Roots of Modern Environmentalism*, Croom Helm, 1984. A member of Friends of the Earth and the Labour Party, he is also Principal Lecturer in Geography at Oxford Polytechnic.

Kim Howells is the Research Officer for the South Wales Area of the National Union of Mineworkers. He has had articles published in the *Guardian* and is widely tipped to be a future Labour Party MP.

Red and Green

A New Politics of the Environment

Edited by Joe Weston

Pluto Press

First published in 1986 by Pluto Press Limited,
The Works, 105a Torriano Avenue, London NW5 2RX
and Pluto Press Australia Limited, PO Box 199, Leichhardt,
New South Wales 2040, Australia. Also Pluto Press,
27 South Main Street, Wolfeboro, New Hampshire 03894-2069 USA

7 6 5 4 3 2 1

90 89 88 87 86

Typeset by AKM Associates (UK) Limited,
Ajmal House, Hayes Road, Southall, London
Printed in Great Britain by Cox & Wyman Limited,
Reading, Berks.

British Library Cataloguing in Publication Data
Red and green: a new politics of the
  environment.
  1. Environmental policy
  I. Weston, Joe
  320   HC79.E5

ISBN 0 7453 0147 9

Contents

Most books about the environment describe the ecological costs of modern society. Yet they often neglect a very human social cost. Every single day over 40,000 children, under the age of five, die because of hunger and poverty. This book is dedicated to today's 40,000.

Introduction

Almost, it appears, without questioning why, the left in Britain is attempting to climb aboard the green bandwagon, thus joining both the SDP and the Tories in the race for 'green credibility'. Meanwhile the greens themselves are divided in an almost incomprehensible debate between the 'red-greens' and the 'green-greens'. All, it would seem, want to be green, yet few, when it comes to it, can describe what being green actually means. Does it mean, for example, having a concern for the environment? If so, what's so special about that? Surely everyone has, to varying degrees, a concern for the environment: after all, the environment means the physical and social surroundings in which our lives take place. Or does being green mean, as I believe it does, having a concern for the Earth's ecology and for 'nature'? If so, to what extent should that concern override others before one becomes truly green? Should, for example, our concern for nature extend to that of the German red-green Rudolf Bahro's? Does being green mean we accept his argument that

> We still regard the ecological crisis as the overriding and broader challenge. The economic crisis and the capitalist response of mass unemployment and dismantling of the welfare state may well change the conditions for the ecology and peace movement. But it would simply be a further victory for the existing order if we let ourselves be pushed into giving priority to the fight against unemployment and the social decline in the wake of the old trade union and left socialist defence strategies. We are not here to defend or create jobs in the industrial system.[1]

If that is indeed what being green means then how can the British Labour Party call itself green? It is, after all, promising a future in which British manufacturing industry will once again employ the millions now on the dole.

While there are obvious electoral advantages for those political parties which claim to have green credentials, it seems rather shortsighted for the left to embrace greenness without fully understanding all the implications of doing so. What is more, the green bandwagon offers very little for people like myself who see in solutions to environmental problems one of the best ways of improving people's lives. For, as we will see, the prime concern of greens is indeed ecology and 'nature'; which means that other, far more immediate environmental problems are neglected.

Living as I do in a principally working-class neighbourhood, as part of a working-class family, I find it difficult to accept that the most important issues which society has to tackle are all related to 'nature'. And yet it is 'nature' – its protection and restoration – which motivates virtually all the actions of greens. Furthermore, despite all the arguments about the social benefits of ecological protection, this concern for 'nature' remains little more than a middle-class priority that is based upon a middle-class under-standing of what 'nature' is.

For me the environment is much more than 'nature'; it is the social, political, economic and physical world in which we live. This means that environmentalists should be concerned with both the physical and the social world. Greens would tend to agree with this, but they would also argue that it is ecology or 'nature' which shapes the social world (or at least should). What we do in this book is reject such ecological determinism and argue that it is the social world which shapes and determines the physical. We believe that environmentalists should recognize that through human activity 'nature' is changed: that which is 'natural' today probably was not 2,000 years ago and will not be 2,000 years hence. This is a view of 'nature' which is in complete contrast with the ecology-based philosophy of green politics and is central to the whole socialist tradition. It leads us to believe that it is not the left which should be turning green but environmentalists who should be becoming red.

With so much poverty and social deprivation within our society it is increasingly difficult to accept the view that what we are faced with today is an 'ecological crisis' rather than a social or economic crisis. Indeed, such concepts as 'ecological crisis' tend to suggest that problems like acid rain, deforestation and the spread of the deserts are somehow separate from the social world. People, although recognized by greens as the cause of such problems, are not seen as the main victims. The victim, as the phrase 'ecological crisis' suggests, is seen as being 'nature' – which relegates those suffering poverty, despair and hunger throughout the world to the periphery of their concern. Yet in fact it is people and not 'nature' who suffer the greatest hardship as a result of ecological damage. 'Nature', after all, will always reappear, albeit in a different form from that which has been destroyed; people, however, rarely live long enough to make up for the disruption and poverty caused to them when other people destroy their environment for personal economic gain. As Fleischman so convincingly puts it:

> Nature will not miss whooping cranes or condors or redwoods any more than it misses the millions of other vanished species. Conservation is based on human value systems. Its validation lies in the human situation and the human heart.[2]

Which is why green politics remains a middle-class phenomenon. To think whooping cranes are important (possibly more so than people) one has to be free of the more pressing human problems like that of poverty.

However, our beef with green politics is much more than a philosophical disagreement over ecological determinism. If green ideas had remained no more than a part of the whole mass of different levels of environmental concern, there would have been no problem. But the green perspective has, over the past few years, hijacked environmentalism; green politics has become the orthodoxy for the whole environment movement. The effect of this has been that almost everybody seems to equate the term 'the environment' with 'nature' and ecology. A concern for the environment has, to all intents and purposes, become a concern for 'nature'. This not only makes for a neglect of many other more fundamental environmental issues but has also helped to create the kind of contradictions which Jeremy Seabrook found in India:

> In the upper part of the factory children spray the sandals with an automatic paint-gun, orange and blue. They are unprotected from the overpowering fumes of the paint – you can feel its effects after just a few minutes. Their hands, faces and clothes are stained with lurid colours; the oldest is 16, the youngest 10. Bhavani Plastics have donated a sapling in a painted oil-drum to improve the environment; it stands on a heap of rubble and stones against a background of barbed wire.[3]

Seabrook may be talking about India but we can find exactly the same kind of contradications here in Britain. There are councils which plant a few trees to enhance the environment while their tenants live in the most appalling housing conditions. And we have a central government which appoints a special 'green Minister' to tackle ecological decline while the problems of poverty and street violence go unrecognized as environmental issues.[4]

Yet it must be stressed that this rejection of green politics does not mean we now believe that natural resources are infinite or that industry can continue polluting the atmosphere with lead, toxic chemicals and radioactivity – far from it. For not only does pollution produce serious health problems for people – especially for the poor who cannot move out of the worst affected areas – but, as Bahro has argued,[5] industrial production, based upon the wasteful misuse of fossil fuels and finite resources, condemns working people to a lifetime of continuous alienating labour. Locked into the capitalist economics of profit and loss and the need to maximize financial returns from every process from extraction to production, it is those who labour in mines, factories and mills who pay the true price of scarcity.

So what we are objecting to here is not the issues that greens take up; it is the issues they neglect as a result of their narrow interpretation of the term 'the environment'. And these tend to be issues which have far more relevance to the lives of the mass of humanity than does wildlife conservation. Furthermore, when addressed in the same campaigning style as greens use to protect hedgerows, the social environmental issues bring one into closer conflict with the real cause of all environmental problems.

When tackling acid rain, lead pollution and nuclear power it is simple (and simplistic) to see their cause as 'industrialism'. But that interpretation hides the real cause of these problems. When addressing issues of the social environment, like poor housing, economic inequality, political power, street violence, and so on, we discover that our analysis has to be far more complex. What we find is that behind virtually all environmental problems, both physical and social, is poverty. This is the poverty created by an economic system which now permeates the whole globe and which caused ecological and social damage even in its pre-industrial phase. That system is capitalism. As a world economic order it links all those who suffer inequality and poverty, whether they be the poor of America who live side by side with absolute wealth, the factory worker in Soviet Russia whose work produces a profit for the country's elite to spend on imported luxury goods, or the peasant farmer of the Third World whose life is becoming increasingly dominated by the cash relationships imposed by international market forces.

It is the accumulation of wealth and its concentration into fewer and fewer hands which creates the levels of poverty that shape the lives of so many people on our planet, thus making it a major determinant of the environment which people experience. It is poverty which forces people to place their own short-term interests above the long-term interests of the Earth's ecology. It is the economics of profit and loss, seen only in cash terms, which lies behind all our environmental problems, from the inner-city decay of Britain to the destruction of South American rainforests. Indeed, although greens lay so much of the blame on industrialism, some of the most pressing of the world's ecological problems – like desertification and deforestation – are more a result of capitalist agriculture than they are of industrial processes.

It is time that greens accepted that it is capitalism rather than industrialism *per se* which is at the heart of the problems they address. It is time for them to redefine what they mean by 'the environment' and begin to take up issues of more relevance to ordinary working people. Yet this is not to say that they need be acquiescent towards the present Labour Party or the rest of the left in Britain. For just as greens need to move beyond their ecological determinism, so the left needs to move beyond the traditional parochialism of trade unionism and away from the old-fashioned ideas, still held by many socialists, of centrist political control and perpetual industrial expansion. It is time to break free of the green bandwagon and the old-style politics of labour. What we need now is a social environmentalism which can have real meaning and relevance to the mass of people, an environmentalism which is not held static by ideological dogma or 'party loyalty' but recognizes the full implications of an environmental perspective.

Before you, then, is a book about the environment which is unlike most others. You will find in it no grave warning of impending ecological collapse; there are no 'blueprints' or utopian futures promised here, and we provide no hard and fast rules for people to live by. All the chapters in this book are by individuals who have earned wide respect in their own particular fields. As individuals they have come from different backgrounds and bring with them their own individual arguments. All are socialists *and* environmentalists. All share a belief that there is a need for a far more relevant environmental movement than that which exists at present. We all argue, in different ways, that there is far more to the environment than 'nature' and far more to our problems than merely industrialism.

In Chapter 1 I state the basic argument for the need to redefine environmentalism and present an analysis and critique of green politics. In Chapter 2, Mark Levene argues that it is not only the term 'the environment' that needs redefining. 'Peace' too is a much misused word. It is often associated only with the campaign against nuclear weapons, yet peace is something we *all* – regardless of political perspective – want and are denied. Furthermore, just as we go marching up and down chanting 'ban the bomb', violence against ethnic minorities, women, children and the old has become part of the fabric of our society and thus a major environmental issue.

Technological change has always had a massive impact upon both the social and physical environment. This is no less the case with information technology (IT), which is steadily gaining greater control over our lives and our environment. In Chapter 3 Frank Webster and Keith Lambe argue that IT – seen by many as the way out of all our social and economic problems – is not a neutral development but a creation of capitalism, to be used for the benefit of capitalism. What is more, they argue that to understand IT we must look to the greens' understanding of technology rather than to socialist ideology.

In Chapter 4 Michael Redclift looks at ecological damage and change in the Third World. In doing so he shows clearly that even in this area of environmental concern it is to the social, economic and political environment that we need to turn for both the cause and the solutions to such problems.

To end Part One of the book, Jeremy Seabrook pulls many of these themes and arguments together. In Chapter 5 he describes the environment of the inner city and the forces which shape it. In this chapter we look at the environment as it should be seen – in its social, political, economic and global context. We are looking here at the environment which most people on our planet experience, and the environment so long neglected by greens.

So, in the first part of the book, we have a series of essays which describe the reality of the capitalist system and the environment it has created: the reality of problems today rather than warnings of a 'crisis' for the future. Yet despite this deep concern for the reality of the present this is not a pessimistic work. In the second half of the book we look at the possibilities which do exist for bringing some change in our lives and our environments.

In Chapter 6 David Pepper describes how there is already a great deal of commonality between reds and greens, and how, with some adjustments and a willingness to adapt on both sides, there is a real opportunity for the creation of a new, dynamic movement which could dominate the politics of the future. Continuing in this vein, Kim Howells argues in Chapter 7 that the longstanding jobs versus environment debate – which has so long divided reds and greens – is a false one. He provides hard evidence that possibilities for massive job creation *do* exist in energy conservation. Yet he also argues that time is short and that if the necessary policies are to be taken up they need to be formulated now by an alliance of reds and greens.

In the final chapter I continue the book's emphasis on realism by looking at the problems of and possibilities for a campaigning social environmentalism. Although we face major difficulties, through a 'total community' approach to environmental problems we can, I argue, make some changes to the society we live in. Furthermore, by campaigning at neighbourhood level, on issues which are important to local people, we can become far more relevant than is the present green movement, and begin to change the whole political climate of this country – something which is a prerequisite for real social change.

This book is an attempt to move beyond the destructive 'I'm more green than you' debate of modern environmentalism. It is an attempt to begin the development of a concern for the environment which is much more than a narrow, though important, concern for 'nature'. The arguments put forward here will not be new to those socialists and those in the planning movement who have always seen the environment in this way. But for greens and for those socialists keen to climb aboard the green bandwagon this book will, we hope, make them look again at what the environment really is.

My own 'social environmentalism' has developed, in large part, from the previous work of the people who have so kindly helped to produce this book. I am most grateful to all of them, but particularly to David Pepper who has helped at every stage of the book's development. I have also been greatly influenced by people not represented here but who should be mentioned. In particular Peter Worsley, whose book *The Three Worlds*[6] graphically details the ways in which the environment has been transformed over time. Then there is Paul Harrison's *Inside the Inner City*,[7] a book which describes the environment which we environmentalists have neglected for too long and to our shame. Then there are all my colleagues at Friends of the Earth, one of the very few environmental organizations to have taken up the issues of the social environment.

One more influence on the development of my 'social environmentalism' which ought to be mentioned, although it probably says more about my age and class than my politics, has been the music of Bruce Springsteen. The songs contained on his album *Born in the USA*[8] put into words and music the whole atmosphere of the contemporary western environment. They provide a clear insight into the lives of millions of people as they experience the world of the modern city with all its attractions and contradictions. Furthermore, Springsteen provides a simple message to all – reds and greens – who seek to bring change to the society we live in:

> You can't start a fire,
> Worrying about your little world falling apart.[9]

Part One:

Redefining Environmentalism

'Environmental problems are really social problems anyway. They begin with people as the cause, and end with people as victims.' (Sir Edmund Hillary in *Ecology 2000*, Michael Joseph, 1984, p.15)

1. The Greens, 'Nature' and the Social Environment

Joe Weston

The problem of 'nature'

Early in 1981 Oxfordshire Friends of the Earth (FoE) took a decision which illustrates one of the main problems facing modern environmentalism in Britain. Confronted with Department of Transport plans to extend the M40 motorway, Oxfordshire FoE decided to focus their anti-motorway campaign upon a single section of the route, a section which would require the dissection of Bernwood Forest – thought to be Britain's premier butterfly habitat – and the crossing of Otmoor, an historic semi-wetland six miles north of Oxford. This seemingly unremarkable decision is extremely significant. For in focusing on a threat to wildlife, Oxfordshire FoE had to reduce the amount of time and resources available to them for the pursuit of the other issues involved. The excellent critique of the British transport system – developed by FoE over ten years of campaigning – was virtually lost in what became a campaign to 'save' Bernwood and Otmoor.

All the modern environmental groups which have emerged since the early 1970s, like Greenpeace and FoE, have from time to time been forced to make this kind of pragmatic campaigning decision. As small independent organizations, their fragile financial positions have forced them to court mass support – which in Britain has meant appealing to those whose environmental sympathies lie in 'nature' conservation. Often as a result of the real need to attract funding for campaigns, modern environmentalism has become little different from the protectionist conservationism which it had once attempted to replace.

This is profoundly disappointing, for when modern environmentalism first appeared it did seem to be offering much more than the protection of wildlife. It seemed to be promoting a radical approach to environmental problems, an approach which would create the conditions through which social change would become possible. The launching of FoE in 1971, with the dumping of thousands of empty non-returnable bottles on the doorstep of Schweppes in London,[1] seemed to be an attack upon the very fabric of the capitalist system. It appeared to be questioning the 'right' of capital to accumulate wealth at the expense of society and the environment. Since then, this 'new' environmentalism has achieved very little. Apart from some cosmetic measures to protect wildlife, the pressures upon the environment are as strong today as ever; despite a decade and a half of lobbying and campaigning, that 'right' of capital to pass on its costs to society and the environment is just as entrenched. Its radical image and its recent expansion hide the fact that modern environmentalism has failed to live up to its early promise; it has remained tied to the same narrow concern for wildlife protection from which its founders had hoped to escape.

However, the failure of modern environmentalism to live up to its early radical image goes much deeper than its inability to achieve more than cosmetic wildlife protection. For just as Oxfordshire FoE had all but to ignore the non-wildlife issues in the M40 campaign, so the retreat to wildlife protectionism has allowed modern environmentalists to neglect the most important environmental issues of our age. For example,

> In every city and town, the centres of industrial and commercial activity and wealth, people live in damp, poorly insulated and inadequately heated homes, perhaps sharing with another family or individual a cooker on the landing and a single bathroom. For others it is a matter of living in one room divided in two by hardboard, a gas ring and wash basin next to the bed, a suitcase on the wardrobe, no privacy of sound from the other occupied rooms, and the inconvenience of sharing with the whole house the use of the one toilet which it is no one's responsibility to clean.[2]

John Cowley is here describing environmental conditions in Britain during the early 1980s, a time when poor housing constituted an assault upon the environment of an increasing number of people in this country, mirroring the lives of millions in the Third World. Yet during the same period the mass of the environmental lobby – one of the most innovative and imaginative movements to have emerged for generations – was concentrating its not inconsiderable resources upon protecting hedgerows, butterflies and bunny rabbits. Little wonder then that support for environmental groups remains firmly rooted in the middle class. For modern environmentalism, with its virtually exclusive concern for 'nature', remains irrelevant to those suffering the kinds of environment described above.

Furthermore, this concern for wildlife is much more than simple pragmatism. We cannot get away with arguing that it is the need to attract funds which has alone been responsible for modern environmentalism's preoccupation with wildlife issues. The problem goes much deeper than that; at its heart are the 'ecological beliefs' which underlie so much of modern environmental concern.

For most people in the green movement the term 'the environment' essentially means that which is related to the Earth and its ecological systems. Acid rain, the destruction of tropical rainforests and modern agricultural practices are seen as an attack upon 'nature'. Even non-wildlife issues like nuclear energy and air pollution are seen in terms of their effect upon the biosphere – the Earth's ecology – and the threat to human health that these effects have. This extremely narrow view of 'the environment' not only neglects the social environment – the social, political and economic system in which we live – and the built environment – like the inner cities – but much more fundamentally it is based upon an incorrect assumption of what constitutes 'nature'. For example, if I were to look up for a moment, out of the window down between the council houses, I would see Bernwood Forest. As I sit typing I know that within twenty minutes I could be in Bernwood: a walk which would take me down a lane rich with summer wildflowers, insects and birds. I grew up, and now my children are growing up, in an environment which is dominated by the close proximity of what we like to call 'nature'. That lane, and the forest, obviously had a profound effect on my development and they remain exciting places in which children can play.

Contrast this environment with that of places like Hackney in London, where children play in surroundings which are dominated by noise, violence, danger and poverty. It is an environment where childhood ends early and harsh economic reality stunts development, a place where it can take twenty minutes just to reach the ground from blocks of flats built for financial utility rather than for human need.

Little is said by modern environmentalists about the second of these two types of environment. The first – the British countryside – has been the focus of massive interest over the past few years, yet that lane down to Bernwood is no more 'natural' than an inner-city road. It is a farmtrack, created by humans for human use, to fulfil a human need which has been socially determined. Similarly, Bernwood is managed for its timber; it would not exist if it were not for people who make use of it for social and economic benefits.

To base environmental campaigning on a concern for 'nature' is, then, to ignore the social construction of the environment and the most important environmental problems with which we are currently faced. For it is we, as a society, who shape our environment by deciding which social and economic priorities should prevail;[3] we choose our environment rather than have it imposed upon us by 'nature'. Whether we live in the centre of a large city or on the edge of a forest, the physical environment starts at our front doors, making environmental issues those which are concerned with our surroundings – both physical and social – rather than those which are in some way related to 'nature'.

By looking at environmental issues from this wider perspective we become much more able to understand and confront both the causes and the effects of environmental problems. From this starting point – that our relationship to 'nature' is dependent upon social rather than physical factors – we can see through the smokescreens and falsehoods which hide the true causes of a poor environment. For example, the people of the USA can build a holiday centre with vast lakes for fishing and boating in their deserts, while the people of Africa starve to death in theirs. The difference between them is not a difference of climate or, as environmentalists have tended to argue, of population size. The difference between them, the one thing which above all else determines their respective relationships with 'nature', is their wealth. In the wealthy western democracies 'nature' has become something to enjoy and protect, whereas in the Third World the poor often see 'nature' as something to be feared.[4]

In their neglect of the social construction of the environment, modern environmentalists have selected campaigning priorities which seldom reflect the true scale or the true causes of the world's problems. As a consequence, their movement is largely irrelevant to the mass of humanity. The problems with which most people are now faced are not related to 'nature' at all: they are related to poverty and the transfer of wealth and resources from the poor to an already wealthy minority of the Earth's population, and they are ones which the basically conservationist campaigning of most modern environmentalists is incapable of addressing. Indeed, most environmental problems require an approach which is diametrically opposed to the ethic of conservation; what they require is an approach which recognizes that the environment, as experienced by most people, needs radical and fundamental change, not protection. Rather than conserving the environment in which most people now live, the inner city and the shanty town, need destroying. It is this fact that the present preoccupation with 'nature' seems to hide from the mass of the green movement.

In many ways this failure of modern environmentalism to become anything more than a reflection of a wealthy society's concern for wildlife, is evident in its recent growth. The very fact that it now draws support from such a wide spectrum of political opinion is evidence of its failure to threaten the status quo. All the major political parties now claim green credentials – and can legitimately do so because of the extremely diverse political traditions associated with a concern for 'nature'.[5] If environmentalism in Britain had developed differently this would not have been the case. A campaigning environmentalism, based upon an understanding of the social construction of our physical surroundings, would have been in direct confrontation with the capitalist system. It would have recognized that it is capitalism and the transference of wealth from the many to the few which lies behind the problems which the greens now address. It would thus have become a far more radical force for change.

That the environmental movement did not develop in this way created a personal need for me to reassess my own decade-long commitment to green politics, a commitment which had brought about some very real changes in my, and my family's, lifestyle and which I was reluctant to completely turn my back on. In making this reassessment I looked critically at green politics and what it has come to mean. It was an exercise which proved to me that for my family, my community, my class and the mass of humanity, green politics is all but an irrelevance. It is that admittedly partial analysis that I now share with you.

The development of modern environmentalism

When modern environmentalism first emerged, with the birth of groups like FoE, Greenpeace and the Ecology Party during the early 1970s, the west was reaching the end of a long period of economic stability.[6] From 1945 onwards, economic growth and political consensus in Britain had largely eroded the class-based politics of the pre-Second World War era. The establishment of the welfare state, the expansion of the education system and the nationalization of key public utility industries were seen as both acceptable and inevitable features of a modern industrialized nation. This expansion in the role of the state in turn helped to increase both the size and the influence of the middle class, as it created the conditions under which service sector employment could grow. Meanwhile, higher wages, shorter working hours and improved working conditions for manual labour had, by the mid-1960s, made it difficult to continue dividing society up into social classes.

Because of these social and economic changes the 'middle ground' began to dominate British politics. And it was this that both the Labour and Conservative Parties attempted to win, producing a long period of consensus politics when little separated the programmes of the parties competing for government. This erosion of party differences had the effect of taking many issues completely out of the political debate, creating a political vacuum in which issues concerning a large number of people were all but neglected by politicians. Increasingly during the 1960s this vacuum became filled by protest groups. The issues which concerned them – racism, the threat of nuclear war, the reality of the Vietnam War and the growing evidence of ecological damage – provided the stimulus for political action outside the mainstream of the political system, and gave rise to the formation of political movements which largely replaced the political party as the means through which radical political activity took place during the 1960s.[7] And the pressure group tactics pursued by these groups had seldom been seen on such a scale before. The 'freedom rides' and marches of the US Civil Rights Movement and the sit-down demonstrations of CND in Britain are both examples of the kind of protest style which characterized political activity during the 1960s.

These movements were seldom a serious attempt to transform society completely. More often than not they were simply attempts to force incremental change upon society: they were reformist rather than radical forces for change. However, by the late 1960s some elements were beginning to raise issues which did suggest to them a need for complete and fundamental social and economic change. With the growing economic crisis of the late 1960s some, notably students, turned to the radical left, while others turned away from all the old political orthodoxies and towards what were seen as new answers to society's ills. It is among this latter group that we find the new environmentalists, who were starting to argue that there were links between the social problems of the period and the ecological damage which modern industrialism was producing. These links suggested to them that only a profound change in the make-up of society could solve the problems of racism, sexism, drug abuse and violent crime, and at the same time stop the destruction of the 'natural' environment. This new radical environmentalism became established with the creation of groups like 'Zero Population Growth' and through the publication of books like Paul Ehrlich's *The Population Bomb*, Garrett Hardin's work *Tragedy of the Commons* and the many others which linked social problems to environmental decline.[8]

This new environmental radicalism was very different from the political radicalism of earlier generations. In an affluent society, apparently free of poverty, the focus of attention had become excess consumption rather than the fulfilment of need. Those who now advocated social change did so from a perspective which was critical of society's wealth and not of its inability to tackle poverty. It was the way society made use of natural resources and the rate of population growth which concerned those who, by the early 1970s, were beginning to steal the political limelight.

A great deal of emphasis began to be placed upon the 'threats' to the Earth's ecology by the expansion of material wealth. Environmental issues, that is issues related to the Earth's ecology, became politically and economically important as more and more people came to believe that resources were about to run out; that industrial pollution had reached dangerously high levels; that wildlife destruction was taking place on an unprecedented scale. As Blowers has argued,[9] by the early 1970s, companies which had been causing pollution for generations found themselves almost overnight the targets of intense pressure-group activity. Furthermore, this pressure often came from people who had apparently lived unconcerned by the pollution for many years. From being the local economic benefactors, factory owners suddenly found themselves a target for political protest as a society, apparently free of the poverty of earlier generations, began to look critically at the effects of its new-found affluence.

In this way an interest in wildlife and 'nature' became transformed. In place of the protectionist concern of a wealthy land-owning minority, a new environmentalism called for fundamental social change.[10] It was a radicalism which believed in the existence of an 'ecological crisis': a 'crisis' which had been created by modern industrial affluence; a 'crisis' which required both radical social change and the acceptance that ecological concerns should transcend all others. For example, writing in 1971, Paul Ehrlich and Richard Harriman argued:

So, it is clear that Spaceship Earth is in deep trouble. But the situation is not hopeless – indeed we can probably survive the current crisis and set mankind on the path to a long and pleasant space voyage. We can, that is, if we *dramatically change* the ways in which we treat both our fellow passengers and our vessel [emphasis added].[11]

These twin emphases – 'ecological crisis' and the need for social change – were the dominant themes of early 1970s environmentalism. A whole galaxy of warnings were produced to draw public attention to the 'threats' to the Earth's survival. Morever, this trend was reinforced by the renewed popularity of some old philosophical themes in western thought. Apart from the Malthusian concern for overpopulation and resource depletion, there was also a rebirth of Romantic beliefs in the existence of a 'web of life'. The 'laws of ecology' were used to explain how this 'web' connected all living things to the ecological imperatives of the Earth. People were seen as little more than links in the vast 'chain of being',[12] and so protecting 'nature' became the only safeguard for humanity. It was through these beliefs that virtually all environmental concern became a concern for 'nature' and ecology.

Out of the merger between radical campaigning environmentalism and these philosophical ideas emerged a 'new' political perspective which eventually became green politics. It is a perspective which links Romanticism and ecological determinism with a profound dislike of industrialism. Indeed, behind all the warnings of the early 1970s were constant attacks upon the industrialism which had brought about western affluence. This attack is nowhere clearer than in the influential *A Blueprint For Survival*,[13] the first page of whose opening chapter declares:

The principle defect of the industrial way of life with its ethos of expansion is that it is not sustainable. Its termination within the lifetime of someone born today is inevitable.[14]

The industrial system is seen as having its own imperatives which are largely responsible for the ecological 'crisis'. The emphasis which society places upon economic growth and material progress, for example, is thought to be in conflict with the 'laws of ecology'. Industrial production, with its reliance upon finite resources, is seen as unstable because it does not conform to the cyclical needs of the Earth's ecology, where the 'interconnected, interacting elements are constantly being renewed'. Industrialism is, therefore, seen as inherently 'unnatural', as it depends upon the exploitation of the planet rather than on 'harmonious co-existence'.

Through writers like Ehrlich, Hardin, Goldsmith and many others, the ecological imperative – our supposedly inescapable dependence upon the 'laws of ecology' – became a key concept for green politics.[15] From this belief greens have constructed a whole set of policies and campaigns for the protection of the Earth's ecology. Hence we find the 1983 Ecology (Green) Party manifesto arguing:

> The slow destruction of the Earth cries out for radical changes in our society, in our politics, in our very souls. Until we learn to respect the rights of the Earth, there'll be no guaranteeing the rights of its people. Until we insist on human scale in all we do, there'll be no guaranteeing the rights of the Earth. Liberation and survival go hand in hand.[16]

This emphasis on the unity of humans with 'nature' has resulted in modern environmentalism's continued preoccupation with the protection of 'nature' and the Earth's ecology at the expense of an emphasis upon social problems, even when those problems are clearly environmental in both content and cause. Of course the greens argue that their campaigns do have a human factor in that protecting the Earth's ecology also protects people, and it is obviously true that campaigning against nuclear power and air pollution does reduce health risks. But so would countless other campaigns which environmentalists ignore. For example, the campaign against radioactive discharges from Sellafield has emphasized the possible links between the deaths of about a dozen children from leukaemia over a period of thirty years and radioactive discharges from the BNFL reprocessing plant. As tragic as this may be, that many people – many of them children – die every day on Britain's roads is a fact ignored by the mass of the present green movement.[17] If greens are that concerned with human health, why have they not taken up issues which are more immediate threats than radioactive waste? The reason is clear: radioactivity is seen as a long-term threat to the Earth's ecology – a threat to 'nature'. The principal concern of modern environmentalism is, therefore, not the fact that people die as a result of environmental problems but the effect that human activity has on the Earth's ecology.

Over the past few years, and particularly since 1979, an increasing number of people have come to accept this narrow view of what the term 'the environment' means. Within the groups formed since the late 1960s there has also been a growing tendency to make alliances with green politics – a fact which contributed to the decision of the Ecology Party to rename itself the Green Party in 1985. The reasons for this drift towards green politics by modern environmentalists are doubtless complex. It may be that the shift owes a great deal to the electoral success of Die Grunnen in West Germany, as this placed the name 'green' firmly in the minds of British politicians and the media. It has also gained credence in the light of continued economic recession, with its attendant social problems and pressures, for this has been seen by many environmentalists as evidence of the accuracy of the early 1970s prophecies. On top of this has been the failure of the major political parties to convince people that they can do anything about problems like unemployment without further ecological damage.

For those involved in campaigning environmental politics, these trends, and the often persuasive arguments of green writers, have made green politics very attractive. It is 'new', it apparently rejects the left-right axis of traditional politics and of course it puts 'nature' first. However, for British environmentalism to continue developing in this way – down the road of green politics – would be a profound mistake. Given the liberal/conservative political culture of Britain and their own continued need to be popular, the greens will always be pushed towards the protectionist and conservationist approach of the pre-1970s. And, even more importantly, green politics leads nowhere. It is based upon false assumptions, not only about 'nature' but about the root cause of the issues which it addresses.

Green politics: an analysis

The problem with any analysis of green politics comes when we attempt to define who greens are. On one level 'green' means any group or individual who campaigns or in any other way displays a concern for the environment: everyone, that is, from the National Trust through to the Socialist Environment and Resources Association. This is far too large an interpretation, for it neglects the very real differences which exist between such groups. In reality there are a number of different levels of environmental concern, only some of which can usefully be described as green.

First, there are the traditional conservationists, groups such as the National Trust and the Royal Society for the Protection of Birds, which seek only the protection of wildlife, rural amenity and historic buildings. Secondly, there are the hundreds of single-issue, often local and community-based groups which spring up in response to a specific problem. In this category we find groups such as that which has campaigned against the building of London's third airport at Stanstead. These groups are often far more radical in their campaigning style than are the traditional conservationists. Thirdly, there are the holistic, multi-issue groups which campaign at national and local level. These groups tend to argue for fundamental change in order to prevent ecological damage, often arguing that all the issues which they address are linked, biologically through the Earth's ecology and politically through their root cause. It is, of course, this third group which most often argues under the banner of green politics. However, there are difficulties even here. Groups like FoE and Greenpeace, while clearly within this category, actively distance themselves from the Ecology (Green) Party in order to maintain their apolitical campaigning credibility; others, like SERA (Socialist, Environment and Resources Association), are unashamedly socialist. This means that although they are all part of the wider green movement we must leave such groups out of this analysis. The following is an analysis based upon the work of people who do actively promote the cause of green politics and not on those who simply call themselves 'green'.

At the centre of green politics is the concept of an ecosystem, where balance is maintained through the interaction of inter-dependent component elements. The belief that this is the case in the human social world as well as in 'nature' allies the greens to an essentially pluralist analysis of contemporary society, for pluralists tend to understand society through studying the interaction of social groups and interests.[18] The key figures in the pluralist tradition – people like Bell, Galbraith and Dahrendorf[19] – argue that social harmony is maintained through the free competition of independent, yet complementary, interests.

Similarities between the green perspective and the pluralist school do not end here; for, as argued above, a great deal of emphasis is placed by greens on a critique of the 'industrial society'. This position is clearly displayed in the 'Common Manifesto of the European Green Parties':

> Although Green political initiative has developed independently in each country, we have each identified that the *root causes* of these signals [ecological damage] is the consumer based, industrial societies of the 'developed' world . . . [emphasis in the original].[20]

That term – 'industrial society' – is a pluralist concept used to distinguish contemporary society from orthodox capitalism; it is not a neutral term. For pluralists, 'industrial society' is distinguished from capitalism by the existence of freely competing interests which are not based upon social class. They argue that the class-based society of the classical capitalist era has been replaced by a highly complex 'industrial society' in which economic interests are simply one of many countervailing factors in the distribution of resources. The greens' critique of the 'industrial society' is implicitly an acceptance of that social analysis, and is therefore a rejection of the alternative Marxist concept of capitalism. Indeed, greens reject the Marxist reduction of society into two competing social and economic classes: an analysis which emphasizes the domination of political action by economic wealth.

In rejecting the Marxist position, greens tend to argue that it is industrialism rather than any one social structure – capitalism or socialism – which is responsible for ecological problems. For example, Jonathan Porritt, the well-known green and author of *Seeing Green*, argues:

> Rivals no more, united in their industrial super-ideology, the nations of east and west blithely go about their business of destroying the planet.[21]

This statement not only echoes Daniel Bell's famous *End of Ideology* east-west convergence theory,[22] but also Galbraith's argument that 'given the decision to have modern industry, much of what follows is inevitable and the same'.[23]

Such similarities between green and pluralist ideas can also be found in their respective treatment of social class. Like the pluralists, the Ecology (Green) Party argues that traditional class divisions are at an end.[24] In fact, greens often argue that a class analysis of social, political and environmental issues is now irrelevant. Like many modern pluralists, greens believe that although some social interests may be dominant – like those of industrialists – such interests are not a factor of class, for they also exist in socialist countries. They are, it is argued, interests which dominate because of the characteristics of industrialism and its preoccupation with economic growth.[25] Furthermore, greens believe that the ecological 'crisis' transcends all special interests, class or otherwise.

So there are distinct similarities between a green and pluralist analysis of society. They differ, however, on a very fundamental issue. The pluralist school is basically an advocate and supporter of the 'industrial society': it sees it as a positive development which emerged out of capitalism. The greens, as we have seen, challenge this. While accepting the pluralist social analysis – the erosion of class, the end of ideology and the interaction of social interests – they reject the industrialism on which that society is based. The greens accept the 'industrial society' model as a means of understanding the way in which society operates, but they see industrialism as being inherently 'unnatural' and unsustainable.

This rejection of industrialism is never clearer than in the greens' discussion of the now-dominant social values. Clearly still within the tradition of pluralist thought, the greens place a great deal of emphasis on the role that scientific, analytic and rational thought has played upon the formation of society's dominant ideas. However, unlike Bell – who sees in rationalism and the importance which society gives to experts and professionals the promise of transition to a new post-industrial age[26] – greens argue that rational thought lies behind some of the most harmful aspects of modern society. Indeed rational, reductionist analysis – seen as an intrinsic feature of industrialism – is blamed for the acceptance by society of the exploitation of 'nature'. For Capra,[27] and for many other leading green writers, there is a clear link between the development of science and technology, especially since the seventeenth century, and the generally held belief that humans can and should dominate 'nature'. Capra also argues that industrialism and its mechanistic world view is responsible for the domination of women by men. In 'nature', he argues, all humans have equal proportions of what we now call male and female characteristics – competitiveness and co-operation, rationalism and intuition. With the advent of industrialism and rational science, claims Capra, only the masculine characteristics became valued; this, in his view, brought about the patriarchical society we live in today.[28]

Capra also identifies in rationalism the erosion of spiritual values in favour of secular individualism. Part of being green, it would appear, is the 'recovery' of the 'spiritual dimension' of human existence. This means becoming aware of the spiritual relationship which 'exists' between people and 'nature' and fostering an awareness of 'the oneness of all living forms and their cyclical rhythms of birth and death, thus reflecting an attitude towards life which is profoundly ecological'.[29] This belief in the need to create a new spiritualism means that many greens argue that to achieve social change we need first to change the values of society, and to this end they place a great deal of faith in education – though not by the state. Greens also believe that to bring about the required change of values, people must first be made aware of what Porritt calls our 'enlightened self interest'.[30] This is the knowledge that unless we abide by the ecological laws of 'nature' we will perish; our 'enlightened self interest' is our own survival. They go on to argue that through the promotion of green politics people will become aware of the dangers of industrialism and the fragility of the Earth's life-support systems. This knowledge will then create an 'ecological consciousness' which will pave the way for a complete transformation of society.

These links between green and pluralist thought are of far more than academic significance. An understanding of the elements which make up green politics is essential if we are to assess its potential. And the links to pluralism provide us with a starting point for such an assessment.

Clearly the green analysis of environmental and social issues is within the broad framework of right-wing ideology and philosophy. The belief in 'natural' limits to human achievement, the denial of class divisions and the Romantic view of 'nature' all have their roots in the conservative and liberal political traditions.[31] Yet paradoxically we find that the greens who make this kind of analysis are simultaneously promoting an alternative to the 'industrial society' which is in the tradition of socialism. Greens tend to talk of the creation of small-scale communities which are organized both co-operatively and democratically.[32] This is a theme which runs right the way through the development of green politics, from the *Blueprint* in 1971 to *Seeing Green* in 1984. Equality and full participatory democracy are essential elements of green politics, as is the greens' deep commitment to social justice.

If we add to this paradoxical position the themes of anti-industrialism, the emphasis placed upon individual rights and the call for a new spiritualism then what we find is that green politics is not the 'new paradigm' that it is claimed to be. The elements of green politics are essentially the same as those which have occurred throughout the long history of populism and populist movements.

The direct action of the Diggers during the 1640s, for example, was based upon a belief that there exists a 'natural' relationship between people and the Earth, a relationship which suggested a need to create a democratic society based upon small-scale agrarian communities.[33] Similarly the anti-industrial element of green politics first appeared in the work of Sismondi, whose work *Political Economy* (1815) argued that limits of scale operate in economics which make industrial mass production increasingly less viable as the scale of production increases. For the Ricardian socialists of the 1820s and 1830s, this represented a 'law of diminishing returns',[34] a concept which is just as important to the greens today.

According to Kitchen,[35] a common theme for populism emerged from the works of the Ricardian socialists and Robert Owen. This theme comprised three main elements: 1) an emphasis on labour value, as opposed to capital value, and hence an advocacy of labour-intensive, co-operatively organized production; 2) a desire to redistribute wealth; and 3) a denial of the right to own land. All three elements are clearly evident in the work of modern greens and lie at the heart of the work of Schumacher, one of the most influential writers in the development of green politics.[36]

Central to Owen's beliefs was the notion that the environment determined the character of society: in small-scale communities, where all contributed to the well-being of the whole, co-operation would thus be essential.[37] This co-operation, Owen believed, was in total contrast to the alienation associated with the large-scale, factory-based industrial system. And this concern for the alienation of industrialism is a theme which permeates the whole populist tradition. Proudhon, whose work *What is Property?* (1840) was an attack upon industrialism, argued that the peasant and artisan enjoyed a wholeness of personality, 'an organic integration of productive activity', which was in complete contrast with that of the factory worker. This is clearly consistent with modern green thought which emphasizes a 'need' for 'human scale' production to replace alienated labour.[38] The American populists of the 1880s argued that the 'natural' democratic society of human existence had been destroyed by industrialism.[39] And the prophetically named Green International peasant movement struggled during the 1930s against industrialization in an attempt to retain the rural communities of Eastern Europe.[40] Far from being the 'new paradigm' which 'transcends the old political framework of left versus right',[41] green politics is part of a long tradition in political thought – older, in fact than both liberalism and Marxism, yet encompassing elements of both.

Again this is not simply an academic point. A comparison of the ideas of greens with populism makes possible further interesting and significant comparisons. Kitchen has argued[42] that populism has predominantly been the reaction of a previously independent social group which is undergoing fundamental change. Essentially this change means the loss of a distinct social identity as people become incorporated into the working class. This is true of the Diggers, peasant people denied common land and forced into wage labour. It is true of the Ricardian socialists, principally craft workers who were again being driven towards direct wage labour. It is also true of the self-supporting small farmers of North American populism who were resisting the spread of mechanized commercial agriculture. If we return to the greens we can find significant similarities between their social position and that of the earlier populist movements. For Cotgrove,[43] the mass of the new environmentalists are drawn from a specific social group which is outside the normal economic relationships of capitalism. The work of teachers, social workers, doctors and so on – those from the 'non-productive service sector' who make up the mass of the green movement – is not measured by the same economic criteria as other sectors of the economy. Hence these people have developed 'non-material values' which place a great deal of importance upon aesthetics and the protection of 'nature'. Unlike other theorists – notably Gouldner[44] – who talk of a 'service class', Cotgrove identifies environmentalists as not only a sub-group of the middle class but also as a 'non-industrial enclave' within the service sector.[45]

Outside of the normal cash relationships of capitalism, this social sub-group has its own distinct political objectives, which within capitalism makes its members 'political outsiders'.[46] So just as the populists of old were outside the polarities of capital and labour, this modern 'non-productive service sector' has enjoyed an independence from the class struggles of capitalism. It is made up of neither exploiting capitalists nor exploited workers.

Interestingly and significantly, the factors which brought about this independence began to come under pressure at the end of the 1960s, just as the new environmentalism began to emerge. The economic growth of the 1950s and 1960s created the education, welfare and health provisions which enabled this 'non-productive service sector' to be created. But with the financial crisis of 1968 and the end of that economic growth, these 'political outsiders' began to face the economic constraints of which they had previously been free. Since then, and increasingly over the past decade, education, welfare and health services have all been forced to accept more stringent financial standards. The 1985–6 teachers' dispute in England and Scotland was clearly an example of this trend: an attempt to force commercial standards upon the social provision professions.[47] Furthermore, the service sector as a whole has been increasingly forced to accept the same kind of deskilling, through mechanization, which had previously reduced the power and influence of organized manual labour.[48] This has had the effect of pushing service sector employment towards similar kinds of working relationships as all other wage labour, often producing a greater sense of alienation – for, as Seabrook argues,[49] service sector employment is rarely creative.

Although we must not forget all the cultural and historically specific factors which created modern environmentalism, we can see that the same factors which gave rise to populist movements in the past are back again. The unyielding greed of capitalism has once more caught up with a social group which had enjoyed a degree of freedom from its harshest features. Faced with the threat of lost independence, elements within the 'non-productive service sector' have developed their own political escape route, a route which is not only specific to a particular social group but is also based upon their own experience of society. As 'political outsiders', greens have not experienced modern capitalism in the same way as have those in manual labour. Outside of capitalist relationships they accept the pluralist description of society and build their own brand of radicalism upon that description. Furthermore, they make use of this pluralist myth to become part of a whole host of people supporting what Bellini calls 'The Post-Industrial Rip Off'.[50] This is the advocation of a future in which people become free of the drudgery of industrial labour, in which unemployment mysteriously becomes leisure.[51] The greens believe this future to be desirable and inevitable; it requires, they believe, only the establishment of an 'ecological awareness' to make the transformation easier. Thus, for them, political action is necessary only as part of the process of 'awareness' building; there is no longer any need for a revolution or a radical transformation of society when the ecological future is 'natural' and inevitable.

Green politics is, then, an attempt by a specific social group to come to terms with its incorporation into the social relationships imposed by capitalism. It is an attempt to protect the values – rather then simply the economic privilege – of a social group which rejects the market-orientated politics of capitalism and the materialistic analysis made of it by Marxists. What is more, like those populist movements of the past who were faced with similar threats, greens use 'nature' as the ultimate justification of their cause. They use it as the final 'trump card' to convince people of their arguments – which, in reality, are no more than attempts to safeguard their own ethical, cultural and moral values. As Douglas has argued,[52] this is a practice which has a long history in politics: when political ideas have little more to commend them than the values of a minority, then 'nature', or sometimes even God, is used to provide an unanswerable 'back-up'. And despite such appeals, the world has not missed these beliefs when they have died away. Feudalism died, although thought once to be 'natural'; so did the Diggers' communities and the other populist movements. Indeed, if the greens' 'ecological society' – the democratically organized small-scale community – is 'natural', why does it not exist today or indeed exist in the past? For virtually all primitive human societies had hierarchical and exploitative social relationships. Like the 'industrial society' concept on which they base their political analysis of the present, the greens' 'ecological', post-industrial society is a myth which remains romantic in conception and utopian in design.

It is clear, then, that from such a narrow social base and from such a misunderstanding of the forces which shape the physical and social environment, green politics will find it increasingly difficult to develop any further, let alone become a truly mass movement. It is a political perspective which is specific to a particular social group. As such, it is incapable of addressing the real problems of others, especially of those who have never enjoyed the luxury of experiencing 'non-material values', those struggling to increase their material wealth so that they can escape from the environment imposed upon them by poverty.

Towards a new environmentalism

Because of their acceptance of the pluralist concept of 'industrial society', greens will always fail to identify both the true cause of the problems they address and the problems they neglect. The pluralist analysis has always been little more than an apology for capitalism, a smokescreen behind which the harsh reality of market forces, class exploitation and the perpetuation of poverty has hidden. In falling for this myth, greens have robbed themselves of the opportunity to develop into a truly radical force. The society they wish to replace – the 'industrial society' – does not exist. Theirs is, therefore, a false radicalism. It is an attack upon a society which is itself no more than an illusion hiding a much less benign reality.

Yet despite their movement's many weaknesses, socialists must accept and build upon the fact that, as Worsley argues,[53] the greens still confront capitalism. They may lack the strength of a socialist analysis and suffer from their narrow middle-class base, yet they are implicitly part of the forces ranged against the capitalist system and should be embraced as such. However, for a truly radical environmentalism now to emerge out of the present green movement, modern environmentalists must accept some very basic principles. They must first accept that it is capitalism – and not industrialism *per se* – which lies behind the environmental problems they tackle. They must also see this capitalist system in its true international context – not as some kind of organized conspiratorial system, but as the chaotic economic force that it is. A force which, with the advent of microtechnology – and the resulting ability of transnational corporations to fragment production and seek out the cheapest source of labour – has permeated the whole globe.[54] With everyone, all over the world in capitalist and socialist nations alike, caught up in its web.

Once greens do accept these facts and allow their understanding of these issues to broaden their knowledge of the forces which shape the environment, they will be able to look anew at the way they think about the environment. That environment is not just 'nature' or ecology, but the social, political and economic environment which envelops us all, whether we live in shanty towns, inner cities or desert villages.

Through using socialist principles to redefine what we mean by the environment it will be possible to create a politics which is much more relevant to the mass of humanity than is that of the greens. By changing the way we environmentalists understand and use the term 'the environment' we can at last become a radical movement for change – a movement which will address the issues of the social environment, a movement which will, however, be more red than green.

2. Peace is More than Banning Bombs

Mark Levene

What are the preconditions for survival in the last decade and a half of the twentieth century? One doesn't have to be a peace campaigner to know that precondition number one, over and above all else, is the avoidance of nuclear war. As the scientific evidence mounts on the theory of the 'nuclear winter', so it becomes ever more clear that a nuclear war, even of limited scope, scale or intensity, might presage the final and possibly abrupt termination of all life on Earth.

Having stated the obvious, however, this chapter is not intended as an addition to the already weighty literature on the effects of nuclear warfare. It offers neither prescriptions for how the nuclear arms race – as it lurches into a new and potentially more destabilizing phase, associated with Reagan's 'Star Wars' programme – can be halted, nor how the more general nuclear confrontation between the superpowers can be relaxed or undone. The peace movement has had plenty to say about these issues over the last five years; there is no need to repeat the arguments.

Delineating and expanding on what are the preconditions for survival may not, however, be the same thing as creating the preconditions for peace. Does it follow, for instance, that the hypothetical removal of the greatest common threat to humankind will in itself ensure a more peaceful world? Or, from another angle, to what degree does the peace movement's emphasis on nuclear weapons diminish the actual, non-nuclear wars going on in the world today? Is our immersion and concentration on the one leading us into the trap of attacking the symptoms of one or more maladies and not the causes themselves?

This chapter therefore starts out with a paradoxical premise – a paradox, that is, for the peace movement. By its very name we know that the movement is striving for peace. Yet by channelling its main energies against nuclear weapons it excludes the lives of millions of people who are daily affected by issues of war and conflict. Moreover, and more fundamentally, by exclusively demanding the abolition of nuclear weapons, it has substituted for itself a surrogate for peace in place of its reality. In this way, far from breaking out of nuclear politics anchored on a firm east–west axis, the movement has been almost as locked into it as the cold war warriors themselves. They, the warriors, create new technological fixes, in the form of new weapons systems, to preserve *their* peace. We demand renunciation as the technological fix for *ours*. They conceptualize their conflict in terms of a global, Manichean struggle between warring ideological political systems, the sharp edge of which is the nuclear confrontation. We subconsciously and sometimes consciously fall in with this approach, making *our* struggle for peace cold war-centric, reactive to *their* criteria, *their* latest weapon systems, *their* propaganda hype.

Of course it would be absurd to deny the peace movement the legitimacy of this focus or to claim that this is the whole story. The movement's emphasis on nuclear weapons in this country rests upon the UK's development as a nuclear power, with an avowedly independent deterrent capability dating back to the early 1950s. It was the fact that Britain was a member of this highly select, bomb-testing nuclear club – initially including only the USA, the USSR and the UK, and only latterly France and China – rather than the equally obvious fact that Britain was a major base within NATO for US nuclear-capable bombers, submarines and briefly missiles, which provided the impetus for the creation of the Campaign for Nuclear Disarmament (CND) in 1958. Based on the perception – very much in the liberal, non-conformist tradition – that Britain could by a unilateral renunciation of her own nuclear weapons do something to halt and then reverse the superpower nuclear arms race, CND quickly developed as a single-issue mass movement with unilateralism as its main plank. And when twenty years later the movement went into its second big phase, this time sparked off by the decision to introduce US ground-launched Cruise missiles, unilateralism re-emerged as its primary strategic goal.

There is an interesting and important comparison here, for the Cruise decision affected not only Britain but also four other West European countries in the NATO alliance: West Germany, the Netherlands, Belgium and Italy. These countries had no independent nuclear deterrent of their own and thus had no main peace organization, such as CND, dedicated to a unilateralist approach. Instead, and as a norm in each case, what were built up from disparate organizations and groups, some with very limited objectives, some setting out from a much broader 'peace' perspective, were coalitions or series of coalitions unifying around an anti-Cruise (and in West Germany anti-Pershing II) consensus.

Thus, while the movement in Britain in the 1980s already had a firm pre-Cruise tradition which conferred on it certain organizational advantages in the form of CND, it was also handicapped by a predetermined, and essentially Anglocentric, view of the nuclear arms race which was not greatly relevant to its natural allies on the continent, who tended to view the issue in much wider European terms. It is interesting, therefore, that in Britain in the Cruise era it has tended to be on the periphery of CND rather than from deep within its structure that broader, less predetermined and more flexible approaches both to campaigning and to general perspective have arisen. Of course, considerably predating CND there already existed in this country traditions of radical, often pacifist, dissent. These traditions, strongly associated with the labour movement or the nonconformist sects – most particularly Quakers and Methodists – naturally fed into the development of CND while maintaining their own broader peace perspective. They re-emerged as important post-1980 elements of the peace movement matrix, providing focuses for the creation of groups such as 'Christians for Peace' and the labour and trade union elements within CND. More significant, however, has been the effervescence of groups outside these traditions, groups which brought to the movement a fresh sense that what is at stake is not simply the question of nuclear weapons *per se* but, more fundamentally, the way in which political and economic forces in the world today exert control over people's lives.

It was this awareness – that nuclear weapons are, so to speak, only the tip of the iceberg, that what is really the issue is how people can break loose those bonds and reorder society and the relationship between societies – which helped give the movement of the early 1980s much of its vitality. And this fresh force has operated on a variety of levels and in a number of ways.

At its most intellectual level has been European Nuclear Disarmament (END), which has sought to set aside the traditional myopia of the 'little Englander' approach and to recognize that the nuclear modernization issue is a trans-European one affecting peoples' lives on both sides of the Iron Curtain. Linking its call for a Nuclear Free Europe to the dismantling of the European military and political blocs, END moved and continues to move 'beyond the Cold War' of E.P. Thompson's famous cancelled Dimbleby lecture, to interrelate the issues of weapons, freedom and social justice in both a European and ever-widening global context. However, while END's contribution to the debate within the national and international gatherings of the peace movement has been an important one, it is hardly known outside of it.

The same cannot be said of the Greenham women, following the creation of their camp outside the proposed US Cruise missile base in September 1981, nor of the large number of peace camps which proliferated at speed, very much on the basis of the Greenham example, during the following year. Particularly in their first flush, these camps received wide media coverage, not simply because of their opposition to Cruise and to American bases in general but because they seemed to be acting and working out actual alternatives to the twentieth-century urban norm. They became briefly, in effect, little islands of emancipation and liberation whose counter-culture emanated outwards through the network of peace groups who acted as their support systems. And when in December 1982 40,000 women 'embraced the base' at Greenham, not only did this signal a potent challenge to the NATO decision-makers but it also, perhaps for the first time, impinged on a wider public consciousness that the emancipatory politics of women was here and here to stay.

These developments were imbued with and often subsumed within a strong green consciousness and ethic. The organizational and tactical emphases on consensual decision-making and grassroots democracy, combined with a commitment to non-violence and non-violent direct action to the point where the latter had become practically a creed in its own right, extended way beyond those individuals who were active members of green CND or who had come into the peace movement through environmental politics and opposition to nuclear energy in the late 1970s. By the time of the last major confrontation with the Cruise programme, at Molesworth in the autumn and winter of 1984–5, the greens had become not only an integral element in CND but also an important factor in the wider peace movement network.

These groupings both within and without CND showed an ability to transcend nuclear politics and to develop programmes of action intended to convey not simply opposition to nuclear militarism but alternative designs for living. Whether these pro-grammes had a wider social relevance is, however, another matter. Of course it is always difficult, so close to the time, to quantify how a social-cum-cultural current from within a particular stratum of society does or does not affect the surrounding ones. It would seem, for instance, that the highly significant role of women in sustaining the 1984–5 miners' strike did have definite cross-references to the Greenham model. But a model for action may not necessarily entail taking aboard the political baggage as well.

The fact remains that nuclear angst and hence sympathy towards mainstream peace politics in the UK has – in spite of the support of key trade unions and the Labour Party – for the most part been the preserve of the educated, white middle class. It is from within this social stratum, not elsewhere, that the new, radical, libertarian and green offshoots have made their appeal and struck roots. For the majority of people whose lives are dictated by the daily round of exhaustive manual or menial labour and drudgery, the threat of nuclear annihilation remains remote; for them the more immediate and more tangible problems of unemployment, bad housing conditions and racial or sexual harassment make the green peace options – still essentially bound within the nuclear straitjacket – painfully escapist or obscure.

For the past five years the peace movement has coalesced around the issues of Cruise and to a lesser extent Trident missiles. Given that all five of the European deployment countries have in principle accepted Cruise, the relevance of this issue is now waning, while there are factors, we shall suggest, which do not necessarily give an anti-Trident campaign a wider social appeal. The peace movement, then, has hit the doldrums, is bereft of a solid peg upon which to hang its strategy and currently lacks the momentum with which to inspire its erstwhile activists to further years of participative campaigning. It is this sense of interregnum, with real political change still some distance away and a strategy against Star Wars and post-Cruise weapons systems less easy to identify and develop, which gives the peace movement good cause to reconsider and re-evaluate what it is about and where it is going. An essential part of this must be to relate itself to the social environment in which people live and work in this country and abroad; in other words, to move beyond the politics of survival alone and towards a wider politics of peace. Both reds and greens already have well-developed perceptions of what this wider peace might entail, but they have tended, perhaps necessarily, to subordinate them to the narrower strictures of nuclear politics and unilateral disarmament. Nuclear politics cannot be jettisoned. Nonetheless it is time to redress the balance.

There is a photograph of a black American military policeman standing in front of the entrance to Brize Norton airbase in

Oxfordshire. Above him, emblazoned in big lettering, for all the world to see, is the sign 'PEACE IS OUR PROFESSION, United States Air Force'.[1]

Clearly peace means different things to different people. 'Peace talks' conjure up images of Reagan and Gorbachev, Scargill and MacGregor, Sir Keith Joseph and the NUT leaders. They grimace and smile at each other for the cameras, yet the public know all too well that, given half a chance and provided nobody was looking, they'd be at the other's jugulars. Reminders of Chamberlain's 'Peace in our time' speech send cold-war warriors spluttering for their machine-guns. Villagers near the bases at Greenham and Molesworth implore peace campers to 'leave us in peace', and sometimes local vigilantes implore them more forcefully. 'Can't I have a minute's peace' is the last plaintive cry of the harassed parent, forewarning for the unfortunate child who refuses to desist, the threat of punishment to come. Peace then is desired by all, is on everybody's lips, is part of every politician's PR kit, is a cliché, a hyperbole – is, in short, one of the most misused, abused words in this and most other nations' vocabularies. It is not surprising, therefore, that when we look at the history and language of international politics, we find that references to the word peace tell us only half a story.

Europe, say the history books, was at peace between 1815 and 1854 – even longer still, if we discount the Crimean War. Yet students of the period know that it was a time of tremendous turbulence, revolution and state coercion. We too have had peace, say the leaders on both sides of the Iron Curtain, for forty years, and they can clearly and correctly point to the remarkable fact that the European continent has enjoyed possibly its longest period uninterrupted by war since the Pax Romana. Yet just as under the Romans, and as in the peace conferred by the 1815 Congress of Vienna, so in 1945 peace had a considerable price-tag attached to it. For the benefit – undoubted and unequivocal – of the dissolution of the Nazi 'New Order', Europeans paid by having their peace not only imposed from above, but also in part from outside their continent. This imposition was perhaps at its most cynical in the secret Churchill–Stalin accord of 1944 when, treating the continent like a giant chessboard, the two leaders divided it up into western and eastern spheres of influence, giving each other, literally, points out of 100 to determine who got what. If, as an extension of this, the powerbrokers of Yalta and Potsdam decided that the Russian border had to be moved several hundred kilometres westwards, thereby incorporating many thousands of unwilling Poles into the Soviet Union, they were an unfortunate casualty. If, in turn, Germans had to evacuate territories in which they had lived for many hundreds of years, in order to compensate the Poles, that again was simply another fact of political life.

The nature of the peace and hence of the political, economic and social framework of the post-war continent was, in other words, for the most part not the prerogative of the peoples who had been bombed and orphaned, and endured turmoil, dislocation and misery for six years, but only of those parties who at that time had the most military power at their disposal.

It would be foolish with hindsight to suggest that it could have been much different. The alternative to Allied victory would have been the perpetuation of some or all of the Third Reich's version of peace which, for non-'Aryan' Europeans, could only have meant either extermination or an abject and racially based servitude. And victory in the Second World War, like any other, inevitably conferred upon the principal allied protagonists the legitimacy to carve up the spoils and, if so be it, to fall out over them too!

The point is, however, that this sort of peace can only be seen in a very qualified way, as a kind of balance sheet in which the benefits have to be set against the penalties. Yes, the impulsive recourse to war between Balkan states, between France and Germany, and Germany and Poland has been prevented by the post-1945 political framework encompassed within NATO and the Warsaw Pact. Yes, there has been in both east and west, albeit at different rates and in distinct ways, economic recovery and development. Yes, there is in the west some freedom, in the east, some social justice. But what of the social and political oppression which also characterizes much of the east and some of the west? What of the artificial economic, political and cultural divide? Above all, what of the great, seemingly geological yet man-made fracture down the middle of the continent which symbolizes not peace but only an absurd and illogical hostility engendered between Europeans as the continuing legacy and price they had to pay for the fact that the Americans and Russians won the war?

If peace in Europe can be maintained only by the largest and most lethal concentration of nuclear and conventional weapons in the world today, there is clearly something wrong with our conception of it – just as there is when Atlanticist or pro-Soviet apologists manage to omit freedom or social justice from their balance sheet.

Greens, of course, implicitly reject this approach. For Jonathan Porritt 'Peace is indivisible',[2] a view which conjures up a conception of an inalienable right which no man or woman can deny to his or her neighbour. In these terms, social and political conflict which results in war should not be allowed to happen in the first place: a statement of principle which cannot be faulted. Applied to nuclear weapons this absolutist rejectionism is not only principled but utterly pragmatic, echoing Martin Luther King's famous dictum 'It's no longer a question of violence or non-violence but of non-violence or non-existence.'

There is, however, a paradox here. Because nuclear war hasn't happened yet, we are – in its terms – still at peace, although we know full well that the consequences of its outbreak would not give us latitude for a second opinion. If this is the only criterion, it is easy enough for peace campaigners, green, red, even blue, to be absolute in their condemnation, to shout plague on both your (superpower) houses and to feel they have not been party to the slightest degree of self-deception. But a problem arises as soon as we start to consider non-nuclear wars or near-wars, wars which are going on right now outside Europe and which are likely to go on into the foreseeable future. In many of these conflicts not only is there no immediate likelihood of a nuclear element but even conventional superpower military involvement may be indiscernible or even tenuous.

In all these non-nuclear wars, however, whether linked to the superpowers or not, the origins of conflict are usually complex and the outcome rarely more than a resting place, representing not indivisible peace but simply the balance and disposition of forces at that particular time. In other words, we are back, as with Europe in 1945, with the qualified balance sheet. But if this is the case, how are peace campaigners who start out from a position of principle to come to grips with piecemeal and essentially pragmatic courses of action which are both part and parcel of and the sequel to actual war? Closeted as we are in an island where there has been no foreign military occupation (at least not by force) for nearly 1,000 years, where no war has been fought for over 240 years and where all our subsequent wars have been fought in somebody else's backyard, are we in fact equipped really to understand what it all means? Can we face up to the fact that picking up the pieces from current wars in the Third World may require us to make difficult choices which are often less than perfect?

If we are at all honest in our desire for the common peace of humankind we have to recognize that it cannot be created by some magic sleight of hand which at a stroke wipes out all the economic, political and military factors which inhibit it or which we do not like. And if it is a peace which is also about freedom and social justice then it will, as in the past, have to be struggled for. The yardstick of what we do in that struggle, for instance in relation to nuclear bases in this country, may be neither applicable, relevant nor helpful to the Third World.

The mere fact that we can make choices about who we do or don't support in the Third World confers upon peace campaigners in this country an unusual privilege. We have the choice to speak out against social injustice and oppression and for peace and freedom. We may even sometimes have a limited effect. The choice does not exist for the Guatemalan, Kurd, Afghan or Ethiopian whose social environment is the conflict; who is conscripted, forcibly evacuated or simply caught in the crossfire. For these people a decision to resist is not a breakthrough to liberty. It is simply the continuation of a life sentence of insecurity and fear, or probably violent death, which would have been their normal lot had they stayed put and faced the consequences. The reality and appalling lack of choice involved in such conflict is so alien and removed from most of the western peace movement's immediate – I emphasize immediate – experience that, if anything, we shut it out. Like the cold war warriors we see only what we want to see, what fits into our preferred ideological prism, and dismiss or ignore what doesn't square with it. And for the most part what we see is 'nuclear'. The point is forcefully put by Eqbal Ahmed:

> The disarmament movement in Western Europe and the United States is, by and large, ahistorical, technocentric, nuko-centric, ethnocentric, phobocentric. It is so obsessed with the technology of war, specifically nuclear war, that it ignores the causes of it. By viewing the arms race as an aspect merely of superpower rivalry and ideological psychopathology, it misapprehends the nature of the Cold War, and embraces the erroneous assumption of bipolarity. By focusing exclusively on the white triangle – the United States, Europe and the USSR – it bypasses the ignition points of nuclear conflagration. By concentrating primarily on nuclear weapons, it overlooks the fuelling functions and trip-wires of the conventional arms race, and the escalating weapons sales to the Third World.[3]

Early in 1985 the National Peace Council put together a rough sketch list of the current armed conflicts or potential conflicts around the globe. It noted five wars between nations, twelve major wars of liberation and a powder of minor ones, thirteen civil wars, sometimes with an element of liberation struggle, and four simmering conflicts with no fighting at the present time. It did not include South Africa which has taken on a more prominent profile since then, nor longstanding disputes such as the Indian/Pakistani confrontation over Kashmir, the Palestinian/Israeli conflict, Turkish/Greek antagonism focusing particularly on the Northern Aegean, nor the longstanding Sino/Soviet border disputes.

There is a unifying factor in all these conflicts, one which does link them to superpower rivalries, and that is armaments. Armaments, primarily from the United States and the Soviet Union, have been unloaded in such quantity onto the world market that there is hardly a self-respecting guerrilla army let alone sovereign state which does not have its arsenal of M-16s, Armalites, Kalatchnikov assault rifles or Katyusha rockets, to say nothing of more 'serious' hardware. The consequences of this are, of course, multiple and disastrous. The unloading of weapons fuels tensions not only in areas where conflict already exists but also in others where there has otherwise been no major basis for dispute. The ensuing arms race expands the role of the military in the political affairs of Third World states and legitimizes the creation of juntas who have an occupational interest in the provision of the latest and most sophisticated technology of war, either to keep ahead of their neighbours or to eradicate internal opposition. For the dissenters themselves there becomes no alternative but a recourse to armed struggle, which in turn creates a further demand for the technology of coercion and political control.

The spiralling costs of all this non-productive hardware further distort economies which are already heavily dependent on the sale of raw materials to the First and Second Worlds, necessitating in turn loans from the International Monetary Fund whose borrowing facilities have severe strings attached to them. These strings, euphemistically referred to as 'belt-tightening', involve the cutting of state expenditure and demands for an increase in the production of raw materials for export at the expense of self-sufficiency. They thereby diminish these countries' scope for independent action, decrease their chances for escape from the poverty trap, but paradoxically ensure the continuation of emergency rule by the military, with all the concomitant dependence on continued arms supplies from the sponsor state that this entails. As we move into the late 1980s, the vicious circle set in train by the arms trade is thus becoming a key – if not the key – factor in the marginalization and pauperization of Third World peoples.

The fact that this militarization of the globe is largely, though not completely, fuelled by the superpowers inevitably threatens to submerge Third World regions in their rivalries. 'When you buy an airplane, you also buy a supplier and a supply line – in other words you buy a political partner', goes the famous saying of the Lockheed official.[4] This does not means that the intentions of the two superpowers are identical, nor indeed that the nature of the operation is the same. They clearly differ. From the client nation's point of view, however, military dependence leads to political commitments; in other words, to their being caught up as proxies and protégés in a bipolar struggle of little or no relevance to their immediate needs or concerns. And where once their islands, peninsulas and bays were only landmarks or points of scenic interest, they are now, as determined by their sponsors, vital strategic elements which necessitate the building of air and sea bases to protect them.

The US and Soviet 'scramble' for bases – potentially nuclear bases – around the globe should disturb and anger red and green peace campaigners at least as much as the installation of Trident and Cruise in Britain. First, there is an element of uncertainty in these developments which threatens our survival much more immediately than any European nuclear confrontation. At least in Europe, and I am speaking cynically, the confrontation is clearly defined, with both blocs knowing more than approximately where they stand and who they can count on. In the Third World, however, the situation is much more fluid. Political stability is at a premium; regimes collapse, change course, sometimes even change sides. A regime which is one day pro-Soviet may the next day be pro-American, and its various strategic bases and installations may switch hands too. Witness the complete 360-degree swapping of allies in the Somali–Ethiopian conflict in the Horn of Africa. Or remember Sadat's post-1973 removal of his Soviet military advisers and Egypt's closing rapprochement with the United States. It is this sort of uncertainty, particularly in an area as politically volatile as the Middle East, which could trigger off the final escalation to Doomsday.

That is, of course, a hypothetical point. What should count even more for peace campaigners is what has already happened and is still happening to people, and the environments in which they live, as a result of all these machinations.

There has been a slow – sometimes painfully slow – but developing consciousness, often brought about by greens within the movement, that people can suffer, be exploited or genetically damaged long before the bombs have gone off. To some extent the massive above-ground bomb-testing of the 1950s and early 1960s and the awareness that this was having serious environmental consequences was a galvanus to the formation of organizations such as CND. But it has taken more than twenty years – and only when two women from the Pacific region were invited over by the women's Greenham alliance – for the full impact and consequences of these developments to have struck home.

Since 1946 some 250 nuclear devices have been detonated by both east and west in the Pacific (to say nothing of those tested elsewhere), with inevitably disastrous and hideous effects on people's health – most strikingly on women's ability to conceive normal, healthy children. The detonations these days are under-ground, but this has not prevented the building of bases, the mining of uranium in nearby Australia, or the wider and more general carving up of the area as if it was just so much real estate for military purposes. It is important to realize, however, that these develop-ments are not simply a question of nuclear weapons, nuclear bases, or even nuclear dumping. Taking over areas of the globe for political, strategic or economic reasons – or more usually an amalgam of all three – regardless of the nuclear element, means the degradation and marginalization of people's working and living environments, even sometimes their complete removal.

In Guam, for instance, at the centre of US Pacific militarization, self-sufficiency has given way to prostitution as the only relevant way to make a living.[5] Nearer to home, the leasing of the British island of Diego Garcia in the Indian Ocean for the building of a major airbase earmarked for use by the Rapid Deployment Force meant, in the 1970s, the wholesale expulsion of its 1,800 inhabitants. These people, who happened to be British subjects, might as well have been on the moon so little did their plight affect public consciousness back home. It is an indictment of our society that the Foreign Office chose Diego Garcia in preference to its nearest neighbour because they considered that the eradication of the population of giant turtles on the latter would raise too much of a stink amongst UK conservationists. There were clearly also racial undertones in the Diego Garcia affair. Unlike the Falklanders, the Ilwa were black or half-caste and hence expendable.[6]

What has happened in the Pacific or Diego Garcia is only a

microcosm of the way the globe is being gobbled up by the military-industrial complexes. There is no distinction here between the nuclear and the conventional. Even in the mid-1970s US military energy needs alone were estimated to account for between 7 and 8 per cent of the country's total energy use, while total US military consumption of non-fuel minerals and other raw materials ran at a staggering 13 per cent.[7] The famous 'sacrifice zones' of North Dakota and Montana, sacrificed in order that the minerals in their rocks can be extracted as fast as possible to keep ahead of the Soviet adversary, are now commonplace worldwide. And when all these resources are translated into the technology of modern warfare and actually used, what then? Do we need reminding that in the period between 1965 and 1973 in Indochina the Americans unleashed the equivalent of 720 Hiroshima bombs, some 400,000 tons of napalm and 1.3 million tons of defoliant?[8] That as a result people today still die from the effects of dioxin poisoning, suffer cancers, go blind or sterile, even produce hideously malformed offspring?

Do we really take in the news of modern warfare when it presents itself nightly on our TV screens? Take as just one example the BBC report on 6 October 1985 of the continuing shelling by Syrian-backed militias of the Lebanese port of Tripoli. 'A city the size of Leeds,' the report ran, 'is silent.' There followed footage of untended corpses in plastic bags and listless, gaping people clearly too blitzed and shellshocked to flee. The images of destruction and carnage, of broken-down communications, untended sewage and potential disease, are ones we associate in Britain with the 'War Game', 'Threads' and the aftermath of nuclear holocaust. Yet here in Tripoli it had already happened. While the peace movement in the west wrings its hands about the lowering of the nuclear threshold, facilitated by new dual-purpose delivery systems, people in the Third World are suffering the daily reality of the upping of the conventional ones. The peace movement is not wrong to concern itself with the threat of a Third World War or its potential ignition points in the Third World, provided it takes into good account that for many Third World peoples the war has already long begun.

Having said that, to suggest that the causes of all these conflicts lie with superpower imperialism would not only be a gross simplification but would also fail to take into account several important ingredients. Peace campaigners, when it suits their predilections, have not necessarily been slow to associate themselves with Third World causes. When, for instance, we are faced with a seemingly clear-cut case of a liberationist struggle against a US, potentially nuclear-brandishing, domination, we are always keen to show our affiliation. Nicaragua and the neighbouring struggle in El Salvador are cases in point, though it is clear that green qualms about armed struggle and resistance instill a reserve not shared by their associates on the political left. On the other hand, mention Afghanistan and much of the left retreats into ideological, pro-Soviet justification or steely silence. Third World people, it appears, like the rest of us, must be parcelled up into good guys and bad ones, depending upon where we stand in the spectrum of 'right on' politics.

But if peace can only be attained in Marxist terms through the triumph of socialism over capitalism, or, from a green perspective, by 'a rejection of industrialism and materialism', what do we make of, for instance, the 'forgotten' Iran–Iraq war?

Dire warnings in 1980 that conflict in the oil-rich and strategically sensitive Persian Gulf would spark off an east–west confrontation have not been realized. Instead both superpowers have, for the most part, been uneasy bystanders to this endless war of attrition with its one million-plus casualties. This does not mean that they are not partly culpable for the conflict nor that they do not have an interest in the outcome. Indeed they have a common interest in ensuring that neither side rocks the regional strategic boat by winning – which is why, directly or indirectly, they have continued to pump resources into the conflict. However, the fact that the fuelling of the war fails to conform to any predetermined east–west criteria naturally baffles western ideologues who like to see an explanation for their conflicts cut and dried. Anti-imperialist, anti-Zionist, anti-communist Iran is discreetly supplied with arms and spare parts by Britain, Israel and North Korea; supposedly pro-Soviet Iraq is equipped in large part by the USSR and also by capitalist France. Practically every other arms-producing nation has weighed in, with more interest in a quick financial killing than any other *raison d'état*.[9] Much more bewildering for westerners of all shades of opinion, however, is the way in which the war is propelled inexorably forward by forces which seem to have little relationship to anything in our own superficial experience.

At work here there is, in the case of Iran, a fierce xenophobia and a fundamentalist religious fervour which, we might argue, are reactions to the modernizing tendencies of the US-backed regime of the Shah. But on both sides the nationalistic impulses seem to go much deeper, a legacy not only of statist concepts borrowed from the west but of group bondings which have roots in the region's often turbulent social, religious and political history. Closer to the scene, we find that even this is too simplistic a picture; that there are other conflicts within this larger conflict, notably of minority groups such as the Kurds, who are trying to preserve their identity against the depredations of the Iraqi and Iranian (and Turkish) states. Against all the odds the Kurds keep fighting on for their own small slice of peace, freedom and social justice, despite the fact that their mere mountain-based, peasant existence seems to fly in the face not only of their immediate adversaries but of all modernist notions of industrial or post-industrial society. But traditional bondings such as that of the Kurds are showing themselves, in the modern world, to be neither isolated nor easily eradicable phenomena. Sikhs and Assamites in India, Tamils in Sri Lanka, African tribes throughout their continent: the attempt to create streamlined, post-colonial nation-states on the First World model is weakened by the tenacity and resilience of local identities based on religion, race or ethnic group.

Conflict between minorities and other minorities (as currently in the Lebanon), between minorities and majorities and between nation-states themselves, are, alongside liberationist struggles against colonial, post-colonial and imperialist regimes, as much part of the picture of a world that is not at peace as any avowed bipolar struggle of the superpowers.

Faith in the spirit of a friendly and co-operative network of Third World nations, as founded thirty years ago at the Bandung conference as a bulwark against all this, has to be set against the disputes they have had and the bitter wars they have fought against each other since then: India against China, fraternal China against fraternal Vietnam, the equally fraternal Vietnam against Kampuchea – to say nothing of the perpetration by the latter's government of the most systematic act of genocide since the Second World War. Our picture of our current world must take account of factors, forces and potential political constellations which have received scant analysis either from western socialist visionaries or ecotopians. Where, for instance, is our critique of the rise of fundamentalist Islam, or its possible echoes in the Judaism of the new right in Israel? Or of the muscular Christianity of the 'moral majority' in the United States? We may dispute these developments as retrogressive or reactionary, but what guarantee do we have that they will not be at least as durable as our own isms?

Religion, race, and national, ethnic and class bondings are therefore issues which should be of fundamental concern to the serious peace campaigner. There is no evidence to suggest that because of the common threat posed to our world by nuclear weapons or ecological disaster they can somehow be rendered inoperative. They are, indeed, all around us here in Britain. To dismiss or ignore them is to undermine our chances of transition to a more peaceful society and a more peaceful world.

In this country we do supposedly have a common group identity. We are British, a people with national characteristics, strengths and idiosyncracies and easily identifiable as holidaymakers or business-people abroad. We are proud of this identity, of our traditions and institutions, and we know implicitly that not only is our way of life in the United Kingdom better than that of other nations but that because of this it is worthy of our patriotic defence in times of foreign interference and encroachment. Yet when we speak of the United Kingdom and the British people who live in it, to what or to whom are we referring?

The United Kingdom is in fact shorthand for a historical process of absorption, assimilation and subjugation by one part and one group within these islands over many other parts and groups. War has been the chief instrument in this process, and its main protagonists have been a foreign political-military caste who after centuries of permanent settlement and land ownership – the fruits of military conquest – came to identify with and then applaud themselves as the custodians of the British nation-state. The subjugated were put to work or sent to fight. 'Ethnic' Welsh and Irish soldiers found themselves quelling rebellions in the other's parts. Later Scottish highlanders whose economic and social relations no longer conformed to development requirements were commandeered into new regiments and sent to preserve or expand new imperial dominions. It's all history, of course. Or is it?

The issue of Ulster only sporadically affects the 'mainland' as we euphemistically prefer to call it. We blot it out until Harrods, Brighton, or the Chelsea barracks becomes the target of another IRA bomb. Yet Ulster is a definite legacy and consequence of British nation-state building – it will not go away, or at least not until we have reconsidered and redefined the whole structural relationship between class, state and nation. Which is why we may observe with some acidity that on the specific issue of Ulster – a glaring example if ever there was one of the need for conflict-resolution – there is no green perspective whatsoever, while the left political position is limited to an almost simplistically asinine call for 'Troops Out'.

One could of course argue that to put so much emphasis on issues of nation and state is to miss an essential point of modern reality. Britain, far from being an economically independent and auto-nomous entity, is enmeshed with and highly dependent upon a network of global capitalist operations and production. Wall Street, Strasbourg, the multinational corporation head-office in Dallas, Tokyo or Sydney define what we are today in Britain much more directly and insidiously than does any flagwaving indoctrination or patriotic Churchillian rhetoric. As for any vestigial political independence, the latest *New Statesman* revelations on the secret 1983 US-British logistic plan surely put paid to any idea of that kind.[10] Britain's much-vaunted sovereignty, we now learn, is no more than a cypher for the day when the NATO alarm bells ring and vast areas of this country, and their populations with it, become Ground Defence Areas requisitioned, in effect, for the US war effort.

Paradoxically, however, and in spite of the decline and sub-mergence of the nation-state within these wider complexities, a sense of national bonding, of being British and proud of it, remains not only a resilient form of individual and group consciousness but one which is widely available for political tuning and manipulation. Ironically the anti-nuclear movement in the period between 1980 and 1983 had here a potential asset which it more or less failed to exploit. A *Guardian*-sponsored Marplan opinion poll in 1983 showed that 61 per cent of the population opposed the introduction of US Cruise missiles, while the *Daily Mail* NOP poll claimed a staggering 94 per cent in favour of a British dual key.[11] There is obviously some discrepancy between these two figures – perhaps the latter sample incorporates all those against Cruise *per se*, as well as those who simply objected to lack of British control. But closer scrutiny of percentage results to additional questions in the Marplan poll do not bear out that this vote was in fact anti-nuclear. Seventy-nine per cent of this poll, presumably including a sizeable proportion of those against Cruise, affirmed their support for the perpetuation of an independent British nuclear deterrent. It is true that 56 per cent were, contrarily, also against Trident, suggesting a disenchantment with Britain's continuing involvement in the arms race and perhaps a resentment against the allocation of vast resources to a non-productive and wasteful project at a time of strain on the country's health, education and other public services. Looked at from another angle, however, it could be that much anti-Trident resentment sprang from an awareness that it was not a home-grown operation but bought at a high political and economic price from the Americans.

The underlying theme, therefore, is a nationalist one. Anti-Cruise was essentially shorthand for an anti-American animus while pro-deterrence was another way of confirming Britain's right – regardless of whether it actually existed – to be an independent political entity. This dovetails exactly with the French position on nuclear weapons. Their opposition to Cruise has been insignificant by comparison with other western countries, but then France, unlike Britain, does not have to accept them on her soil. The French thus had no basis for national loss of face or resentment, and indeed Mitterand could unequivocally welcome the missiles to Europe while at the same time having full confidence in popular support for the nation's *force de frappe* outside the NATO (and hence the US) military command structure.[12]

Moreover, in the British case, any residual possibility that latent nationalist sentiment might be captured for the anti-Cruise movement was dislocated then adroitly deflected in 1982 by Prime Minister Thatcher's call to arms over the Falklands. Again we have to assume that if 80 per cent or more (according to the polls!) supported the Falklands War, then many of these were the same people who opposed Cruise.

The gut nationalist response to the war in fact took the peace movement completely by surprise. Jingoist patriotism had lain dormant in Britain for many years and it had become unfashionable – certainly in middle-class society – to assert it too forcefully. The Falklands put the boot entirely on the other foot. Of course manipulation of the crisis to ensure a military confrontation was nothing more than a time-honoured ploy. There's nothing quite like a short victorious war to quash domestic discontent and, obversely, to unite people, comfortably sitting around their television sets, in adulation of their tribal warriors who are so manifestly providing them with the spectacle of British superiority all those thousands of miles away.

Appeals to atavistic bonding of this sort clearly can work. They certainly helped to bring Mrs Thatcher back to office for a second term. But they can also work in other ways. The nation-state variety works well in relatively prosperous economic conditions and for short periods when the common group identity is considered under threat from the outside. But of course some sections within the British nation-state have never been fully reconciled to it. There was always a resentful Celtic 'fringe' whose social, cultural and linguistic ties ran counter to what was demanded of them by the English Protestant establishment, and when the Irish seceded in 1921 it marked the first major crack in the British national structure. The new entity, however, failed to encompass the six northern counties whose Protestant and Unionist majority forthwith closed tribal ranks against the Catholic south-orientated minority. When economic decline in the 1960s underscored the gross inequalities between that majority and minority, there ensued an explosion of tribal violence, fuelled by the numerous historically based reflexes and stereotypes, which has carried through, at various levels of destructive force, to the present day.

The Ulster conflict, then, is the most obvious example of the fragility of peace – and security – within our 'national' framework. But if for most 'mainlanders' the Ulster problem can be distanced through geography, the breakdown of peace within social environments nearer home cannot. The fragmentation of the social fabric of Britain in the wake of industrial collapse, unemployment and disillusionment is no longer an isolated phenomenon, confined to specific inner-city slums, but is becoming an underlying theme in its own right.

Yet with this collapse there has, paradoxically, been a reassertion of values and bondings which hardly relate to any avowed nation-state consensus. Sometimes, of course, they are dressed up in nationalist garb. When working-class football 'hooligans' go on the rampage in foreign stadiums, or closer to home, they are in their terms 'fighting on behalf of Britain'. After all, 'the essence of being British is to be able to fight' or, as one young Chelsea supporter put it, 'all young men do it, upper class men go into a different sort of gang – the army.'[13] Yet supporting with fervour a football club is much more an expression of a local pride of place, a pride in a community whose industrial purposefulness and meaning have in all probability been wrecked by the requirements of late twentieth-century capitalist development. The territorial protectiveness and tribal violence of the football hooligan in these terms is, as Jeremy Seabrook suggests, a representation of 'a symbolic resistance against the disgracing of the regional and the local'.[14]

And it doesn't end with the football hooligan. Throughout the country, miners who have been marginalized in the interests of 'post-industrial technology' and blacks blocked out from the start by a much more deep-rooted and insidious racism have responded with a tightening of their own local, community, ethnic or racial loyalties and bondings. Economically deprived, socially confined and politically coerced, it is hardly surprising that they often take it out on the harsh and unpretty social environment in which they live, or in violence directed against close neighbours who do not share, or refuse to share, that common identity or loyalty.

Here then in our immediate domestic surroundings are issues of conflict which in their own right are as fundamental – certainly for the people directly involved or affected – and as burning as any question of nuclear weapons or bases. Not that the one does not have a direct relationship to the other. Indeed for peace campaigners there is a real conundrum here. Both greens and reds postulate a need for a radical defence policy based on the popular participation of the people, as opposed to the current state-controlled, professionally orientated and nuclear-prioritized one. In the green case, such a policy implicitly veers towards the concept of non-violent civilian resistance as its main plank,[15] while the radical left alternative reformulates the concept of a militia-based and hence democratically organized defence with some reference to the Swedish and Swiss models.[16]

Both conceptions share a common faith in people's will to act co-operatively and together. Yet what chances are there of achieving any such co-operation in a society as fractious and divided against itself as ours and when the tangible enemy is not the Russian but the Catholic or the Asian up the road? Non-violence as a form of defence against the invader is clearly a non-starter when we can't even contain our violence against each other. The alternative idea of arming the population only exacerbates the dilemma. For example, is not the disbanding of the part-time and majority Protestant Ulster Defence Regiment one of the crucial elements in defusing the threat to, and ensuring the safety of, the minority Catholic population?

This does not negate the need for an alternative, credible defence posture. It does suggest, however, that it will remain a dead letter so long as its protagonists avoid the more acute and immediate social crisis. After all, alienation and deprivation do not, as a matter of course, play into the hands of non-violent philosophers. Indeed, quite the opposite happens. As those at the bottom of the social pile become more removed from the narrow but dominant culture of the white middle-class commuter belt, so they will take out their isolation all the more aggressively on things and people in their immediate environments. Local loyalties and identities under this sort of strain do not work beneficially. White working-class loyalty is directed more and more into petrol bomb and other racially inspired attacks on Asians. Inner-city blacks, as events in Handsworth during the summer of 1985 showed, are quite capable of channelling their violence in a similar vein. Asians will respond with vigilante groups of their own. And as the tempo of inner-city brutalization and inter-ethnic rivalry mounts, so too will the clamour for protection from it, for tighter law enforcement, an end to 'kid glove' policing and, if necessary, for the implementation of the whole technology of political control – water cannon, CS gas, rubber bullets and the rest. A totalitarian version of social peace therefore is not only on the cards but also threatens to engulf us with considerable popular consent.

This is not to say that this version of peace will not be imposed from above, nor that it will be anything but qualified. Its chief recipients will be the managerial, technocratic and quasi-feudal classes, those who it is deemed own, run or control our society. They will be protected, their peace, security and weekend country tranquillity ensured. Middle-class, country-loving suburbia will also be protected providing it accepts the ground rules. If, for instance, parts of it dissent against its nuclear ramifications, those parts naturally exclude themselves from the proffered peace and become *ipso facto* legitimate targets for state repression. Self-exclusion is, however, distinct from an enforced quarantine. Lower down the social scale there will be decreasing parameters of choice. White working-class embitterment will be deflected rather than appeased with 'fantasies of national regeneration';[17] their social environment will not improve but at least they won't be manifestly discouraged from taking it out on the ethnic minorities within their midst. For the blacks and Asians themselves, double-standard policing will ensure that, whatever else, their role in the totalitarian peace will be to receive the full brunt of its punishment.

The chimera of a state system which subscribes to the myth of national bonding while excluding and coercing sizeable elements of its own population, and whose implicit xenophobia and racism translates themselves in foreign policy and defence terms into an antipathy for the interests of Third World peoples, save in the degree to which they can be cheaply exploited: this could be the Britain of the late 1980s and the 1990s.

A green-peace alternative, which concentrates almost exclusively on the nuclear aspects of this tendency to the detriment of the social and economic fabric in which it is created, therefore fails in its task. A green-peace must implicitly and explicitly stand for social justice, as much as it stands against political coercion and militarism. This means considering, providing alternatives for and coming to grips with the daily reality of alienation, brutalization and violence which are the symptoms induced or imposed by the social environment in which so many people live.

There can be little hope of real peace if you happen to live at the top of a high-rise block, if your children have nowhere to play except on concrete stairs, in dirty lifts or on the grey and treeless expanses below, where there are no shopping or social facilities, where by dint of the building units themselves there is hardly anyone you can call a neighbour. Nor, even more intrinsically, can there be peace if, as a woman, you cannot walk the streets at night or are the object of physical or mental abuse inside your own home. There is a whole spectrum of domestic violence, primarily of men against women – though as a spin-off of this, against children as well – untouched upon here. But it too is an inextricable part of our social fabric and hence an environmental issue.

If social justice, then, is part of a transition towards a green-peace, it must lead, insofar as this is impossible without a radical reallocation of financial resources and hence a redistribution of wealth, to a growing nexus between radical red and green politics. Almost by definition there can be no social change without challenging the capitalist system which underpins the *status quo*. This chapter, however, has not been about capitalism *per se*, but rather about the context in which it operates, namely the nation-state. And in the degree to which traditional left politics has been lukewarm about challenging this structure, there is scope for the development of a major and distinctly green perspective.

Much of the traditional Marxist and non-Marxist left is primarily geared towards the assumption of state power as the most effective path towards the erosion of capitalism. But this also carries with it the certainty of being party to its inbuilt structural violence. It is not surprising to note therefore that the Labour Party, at the time of the Falklands War, collectively failed to raise its voice in protest, nor that its own non-nuclear defence option is predicated on the continuation of a state-controlled, national and professional army. For the Labour Party, as for its mainstream rivals, questioning of national state cohesion is anathema. Witness this in microcosm in, for instance, its vituperative denunciation of proposals for separate Black Sections within it. Yet if, as has been suggested, nation-state bonding is not only underpinned by the recourse to war or the threat of it, but is also structurally inimical to major sections of the population, there is surely an urgent requirement for a major redefinition of what we mean by it.

Almost subconsciously greens are in a position to do this. Their whole philosophy starts out from the notion that 'small is beautiful', that local communities are the best judges of their own needs and how best these can be met, that wider society should simply be an amalgam of these different communities and be built up from the grassroots, not imposed from the top down. Green politics therefore implicitly rejects the nation-state, sees virtues as opposed to catastrophe in its fragmentation. The challenge is how to channel these currently explosive tendencies into beneficial, non-violent ones.

Part of the answer must surely be to encourage local ethnic, religious and communal diversity as bondings which are meaningful and relevant, rather than as a social embarrassment and a political aberration. As will be argued in Chapter 8, people who recognize themselves as part of a local, socially useful and productive unit or identity are less likely to be alienated from it and more likely to behave responsibly – dare one say, caringly – towards the people and the environment around them. In political terms what we are talking about is not only massive decentralization but also, to make this approach workable, a concomitant reallocation of economic resources from the central to the local. Structurally this must mean wiping out the social, racial and geographical inequalities which characterize the present system. Psychologically it means replacing the bellicose and essentially artificial macho-chauvinism of the jingoist flagwavers with a local, homespun and essentially feminist-orientated patriotism that is based on *la patria chica* – the native hearth, as it is called in Spanish.

Such a redefined social order would not necessarily spell the end of the political unity of Britain. But it would be a unity of a different sort, a unity composed of many different parts, a unity in diversity. This is not complete moonshine. Other countries engage some of these elements in their actual political structure. Social peace in Malaysia, for example, is premised on the multi-ethnic, cultural and religious nature of its thirteen-state federation. Nearer to home, what we call Switzerland is none other than a confederation of linguistically and culturally divergent yet self-governing cantons. Yet not only does it have relative social peace but it is also able to convey a credible and non-aggressive defence posture based almost exclusively on its non-professional, countrywide militias.

A similar type of confederation may not just be relevant and ultimately a prerequisite for a benevolent version of social peace, but it might, paradoxically, extend rather than diminish the territorial boundaries within which it operates. If, for instance, Wales, Scotland and the six counties of Northern Ireland were themselves self-governing units composed of several equally self-governing cantons, and each was a thoroughly equal partner in a British 'confederation', not only would the historical cause of the Ulster Unionists be completely disarmed, but it might even be difficult for Eire to resist inclusion within it. Moreover, as such a redefinition developed, so too would its defence and foreign policy implications. Much of the way towards achieving peace in the Third World, as Rudolf Bahro has repeated many a time, is at home.

The great question is, of course, how? War has been endemic for millennia, and though in the age of the thermo-nuclear bomb its frontiers have been extended into the potential area of planetary destruction, its causes cannot simply be negated or neutralized by appeals to scientific logic, human reason or morality.

Of course there is a significant section of the peace movement which does put its faith (paradoxically) in these paths. There is, for instance, a common argument that because the course of history has been unquestionably, unalterably changed by the bomb, we must change accordingly, put aside our petty feuds and differences and work for one common goal: the path of human and planetary survival.[18] Much of this tendency is channelled into arguments for strengthening the international framework, most obviously the United Nations, in which diplomatic peacemaking and dialogue can operate, and the approach is often extended into direct appeals to the rationality and statesmanship of world leaders. One cannot deny that this path does have a certain morbid commonsense. Reagan, Gorbachev and the members of their associated nuclear club do after all have vested in them the power of planetary nemesis. In the final analysis it may be that an appeal of this sort may be the ultimate, indeed the sole, collective act of humanity.

But if it is peace rather than simply survival which is the issue, putting our faith in leaders, governments and hence state structures has one tiny flaw. They are part of the problem. To confirm their sole prerogative in peacemaking is to accept not only the imposed peace but also the peace which is the other face of war: the peace of divide and rule, of peace for some and not others, for the rich not the poor, for the haves not the have-nots, for men not women. And this applies economically, socially, ethnically, locally and globally. Moreover, and more intrinsically, this qualified peace contains within it the seeds of a new cycle of violence and destruction, directed if not externally, with the assistance of false national bondings, to the 'enemy' without, then internally to the ethnic, religious or ideologically subversive fifth column within.

Breaking out of this cycle of violence is the real long-term challenge to the peace movement. We have suggested that this cannot really be achieved without fundamentally redefining and then remodelling the framework of our own society. The Marxist-Leninist disciple of course has a simple answer; it is to put one's faith in historical inevitability and the proletarian class which is its agent. His or her dilemma is not only that there is no hard evidence to suggest that the state apparatus and its capitalist allies are in danger of relinquishing their hold but that the occupationally declining British proletariat is for the most part quite inured to accepting this, for better or worse, as an unretractable fact of life. A more green-orientated response is to channel one's energies into non-violent direct action, invariably at or over the wire of innumerable nuclear bases and installations. Though the protagonists of this action generally have fewer illusions about what they can achieve and design their actions to be primarily symbolic, there is again little evidence to suggest, in the aftermath of Cruise arriving at Greenham, that this proceeds from a wide, let alone increasing, popular support base. Indeed, for the majority of the population incomprehension remains the order of the day.

The fact that nuclear installations are designed to be physically out of sight and hence collectively out of mind, even when they are literally just up the road, gives to this type of non-violent direct action an important and legitimate function: namely to keep the bases in the public mind and public gaze. There is, however, a very real danger that by focusing exclusively on this area to the detriment of others, greens will not only dissipate their energies against what is after all the most formidable bastion of the military-political structure but that they will also distance themselves further from the bulk of people whom they are trying to convert.

The process of disencumbering society from the structures of violence and creating peace in its stead may therefore require a much more sober assessment of where we begin and what we can achieve. Instead of buffeting ourselves constantly against the fortifications, we need also to look laterally at the domestic environment – our environment – in which violence is nurtured. In one respect this has a very tangible though not always obvious form. All around us are public corporations and private companies which are involved, directly or indirectly, in the war-making process – not just in producing nuclear triggers or components for Trident submarines, but the whole spectrum of spare parts, computer hardware and electronic gadgetry which are our own 'national' military-industrial complex and the instrument whereby people in the Third World are coerced, managed and liquidated. And beyond these are the administrative and financial institutions – practically all of which have a visible shopfront in our nearest shopping centre – which are their support system. What is needed is non-violent direct action of a systematic and considered kind in the form of boycotts, pickets, non-co-operation and public consciousness-raising, to be directed and focused on some of these bodies. Morever, there are grounds here for the involvement of groups not normally associated with green-style activity, of trade unionists in particular and of state and council employees. The scope for dialogue and debate with people who work in these bodies and with the wider public is almost endless.

What the anti-apartheid movement has so successfully done in terms of the boycott of South African goods can and should be applied, adapted and proliferated in terms of peace campaigning. The results will certainly not be even or dramatic. On their own they will not, for instance, bring about changes of government. But they could be part of a longer-term shift in the social climate, enabling people in their own home environments to come to grips with some of the realities of war-making and how that affects our relationship with people elsewhere.

By implication this approach sets out to view the issues in a broader framework than that engaged in by CND, a framework which consciously or subconsciously tends to dilute the potency of and slow down the impetus towards its single-issue anti-nuclear goal. Yet in Germany peace campaigning both at the local level of the Bürgerinitiativen and in the national arena takes on almost as a matter of course issues of wider, especially Third World, relevance without in any sense jeopardizing campaigns against Cruise and Pershing. Indeed it could be argued that by making a direct link between the costs of the arms race and Third World pauperization, the latter's cogency is reinforced.[19]

The organizational primacy of CND of course makes the British situation distinct from that in Germany. As in Germany, however, the effectiveness of the movement as a whole in this country is founded largely on the resilience and activism of grassroots groups and their ability to undertake local and often autonomous initiatives. The green-orientated groupings at Molesworth, for instance, have attempted to plough the land on the proposed Cruise missile base in order to send the wheat to Eritrea. In this way they have made a connection between the arms race and the Third World and have, by implication, chosen to support a regional and armed liberationist struggle. Similarly women's groups in Oxford have used recent revelations about EEC grain mountains to promote direct campaigns of support for women in Namibia and Nicaragua.[20]

There is no sign on the horizon of a political shift by this country or its west European partners towards non-alignment or positive support for the Third World. Yet peace groups which have undertaken initiatives of this sort are creating their own positive alignment and, more importantly, are doing so on a human scale. On a broader front, the logical follow-on from this should be the creation, with reference to the German and Dutch models, of a coherent national peace network with large organizations such as CND working alongside much smaller ones such as Campaign Against the Arms Trade (CAAT). Such tactical alliances and coalitions can, where appropriate, give a more demonstrative and effective focus to these wider peace issues. In this sense a green-styled counter-culture, which is questioning and practically challenging the foundations of state-imposed and qualified peace, can be built up both at a local and national level. Indeed, some of it is already in train.

But even that still leaves a formidable and fundamental gap which, if left unfilled, will not only ensure that the above will be unsustainable but that their very relevance will go by default. That gap is the present and potentially future lack of involvement of the majority of the population. To win this wider involvement is in part a question of breaking down the clear and obvious resistance of people who have jobs, particularly in the 'defence' industry, who see green-peace primarily as a threat to their livelihood. Even leaving aside a number of key economic, logistical and political problems which would certainly arise should the industry ever be partly or *in toto* dismantled, unless we can offer people a meaningful alternative, the whole notion becomes fanciful. In practice, this means both concentrating a good deal more on what we are *for* rather than on what we are against, and seeking to do this with the direct participation and input of working people themselves. By extension, this means starting not from where people might be (at nuclear bases) but from where they actually are; that is, in their own home environments.

Paradoxically, however, greens are by and large socially, culturally and in the broadest sense geographically not well positioned to do this. Thus while green-peacers' first and most fundamental realignment must be to working people's needs and more urgently still to the needs of those who have been most marginalized, degraded or dispossessed, such a realignment lacks credibility if we cannot involve those who already have a long-term political and cultural commitment to these environments.

By implication, the struggle for peace at a local level, for basic social, economic and environmental rights, and for free ethnic or communal self-expression and identity, must involve some convergence of the red and the green. The indissolubility of peace, freedom and social justice; a green concern for scale and self-sufficiency; a red concern for equality and welfare; a shared concern for community and co-operation: these are the elements which can bring about a durable and sustainable peace in our own home environments. And from here, morever, can be projected through local coalitions of community, self-help and occupational groupings opposition to the organizations and institutions which make peace impossible for people far away. The cross-fertilization of these elements may be the path back from war, 'the last enemy',[21] and forward to a peace created and built by and for the people.

3. Information Technology: Who Needs It?

Frank Webster and Keith Lambe

Anyone who has attempted to present an ecological perspective on technological innovation, and especially anyone who has tried to apply it to the computer communications technologies* currently arriving amidst much delight and zeal, will have found that their necessarily critical and jaundiced views are commonly met with two counter arguments from techno-enthusiasts. The first charge is that an ecological approach is hopelessly nostalgic, yearning for a yesterday of maypoles and Merrie England that never actually existed.[1] The second is that its proponents are hypocritical since the likelihood is that they are themselves surrounded by the results of advanced technology. Heaving under videos, stereos and electronic aids, and secure in jobs – usually in the public sector – paid for out of surpluses made available by the automation of agriculture and industry, how dare they presume to deny the benefits of technology to the less privileged? At that point the debate should be over and the greens dismissed.

Yet the critics of the greens do not stop there. Possibly because English middle-class culture has never fully accommodated itself to industrial capitalism and has long cherished the dream of an escape into a rural idyll,[2] those who favour the rapid adoption of new technologies often try to steal the clothes of the opponents whom they ridicule. They do this by contending that they are the true revolutionaries, that they are most impatient with a status quo which, if overturned in the way they prefer, will lead to a return to the past, to the recovery of a 'golden age' with sumptuous comforts. Their suggestion is that it is advanced technologies which will spirit us to this age of the 'electronic cottage' where forms of domestic production and village-like involvement will be re-established without sacrifice of standards of living. Even the pollution that

* A number of neologisms have been coined for these; for instance, télématique, compunications, informatics. Information Technology (IT) is the favoured term in Britain.

afflicts so much of the world today will be done away with thanks to these new 'technologies that are environmentally sound . . . and non-destructive of the ecology'.[3]

Let us give an instance of this rhetorical trick whereby radical critics are ridiculed whilst their radical credentials are appropriated by those who would have us rapidly and unresistingly accept new technologies. Alvin Toffler, probably the best-known futurist, was dismissive of 'critics of industrialism' who envisage the 'rural past as warm, communal, stable, organic, and with spiritual rather than purely materialistic values', because 'historical research reveals that these supposedly lovely rural communities were . . . cesspools of malnutrition, disease, poverty, homelessness, and tyranny, with people helpless against hunger, cold, and the whips of their landlords and masters'.[4] These advocates of 'pre-technological primitivism'[5] are but a 'small, vocal fringe of romantic extremists' who are 'mostly middle-class, speaking from the vantage point of a full belly', and desirous of 'a return to a world that most of us – and most of them – would find abhorrent'.[6] They are 'future-haters', demented sufferers from the pathology 'technophobia'.[7]

But make no mistake about it, Toffler was no apologist for things remaining as they are. On the contrary, he told us that today's 'institutions crash about our heads'[8] while capitalism is 'tearing apart under the impact of an accelerating wave of change'.[9] And Toffler was not sorry to see the old ways in crisis. Indeed, he was jubilant, because what will replace them is a 'third wave civilization' which will bring about a return to lifestyles that were 'common in the early days of the industrial revolution among farm populations' though now made acceptable and feasible 'with twenty-first century technology for goods and food production'.[10]

Altogether what is offered is a 'practopian future'[11] which looks much like – but is so much more than – the romantic idealizations of the past which everyone is familiar with from evocations of this 'green and pleasant land'. James Martin, principal ideologue of a forthcoming 'wired society', puts it thus:

Local communities in the future may grow more of their own food and provide their own daily needs. They will have offices for white-collar workers plugged into nationwide telecommunications networks. They will have satellite earth stations or other links that provide the same television facilities as the big cities. The local bread and vegetables will be better than those that are mass-packaged for nationwide distribution. Much of the drudgery of commuting will be ended . . . For many the lifestyle of rural communities with excellent telecommunications will be preferable to that in the cities.[12]

The moral of all this futurist propaganda – as if one could have missed it – is simply that

Rather than lashing out, Luddite-fashion, against the machine, those who genuinely wish to break the prison hold of the past and present could do well to hasten the . . . arrival of tomorrow's technologies [because] it is precisely the super-industrial society, the most advanced technological society ever, that extends the range of freedom.[13]

It is not difficult to hear in all this an echo of Marshall McLuhan's faith in an electronic millennium, repeated as another stage in the heroic march of 'progress' bringing still more and better things. Neither is it hard to see in action two axial principles of McLuhanism: one, the commitment to a technical fix to solve all human problems, including those precipitated by existent technologies; the second, an underlying technological determinism which is held to account for all major changes (Toffler's 'wave' metaphor is especially revealing of this).

Socialists and technology

Socialists should not have too much trouble resisting the sophistry of technoboosters Toffler and Martin. Yet in spite of this, it has to be said that in key ways a good many of them share similar assumptions. For a start, there is often a shared antipathy towards greens who are depicted as 'middle-class' wets – Orwell's caricature of the 'bearded fruit-juice drinker' is but one of a long line of gratuitous insults – who are willing to thwart the efforts of the 'proletariat' to achieve riches they have always been denied.[14] More important, there is the left's insistence that technology is a neutral phenomenon which can be manipulated for good or bad depending on who exercises political power – a belief which co-exists (uneasily, it must be said) with the view that technology is the major measure of social progress. Since the days of Marx and Engels and even before, many socialists have raged against capitalist abuses of technology on the grounds that mechanization and automation could be the ultimate means of genuine emancipation. Marx's dictum that 'the way in which machinery is exploited is quite

distinct from the machinery itself'[15] has been restated by socialists
down through the years and with it the conviction that technology,
its bounty properly distributed, is an important means of fulfilling
socialist ideals.[16] At the moment it is the lynchpin for trade union
assessment of and response to new technologies,[17] just as it is for the
Labour Party, which urges that socialists 'ensure that microelectronics is a boon rather than a bane for our people' so that it may
help 'create a historic stage in the development of a socialist caring
society'.[18]

A problem with this perspective is that it leads unavoidably to an
ambivalent technology policy. Not in the sense that it gives rise to
vacillation between alternatives of use or abuse – socialists can
easily enough decide whether technological developments benefit
the rich or the poor – but because of the need to decide, and the
difficulty of deciding, on the extent to which technology of itself
determines social organization. A serious question for socialists is: if
technology is a prerequisite of socialism, is there a degree to which it
subordinates politics to a logic of its own? In other words, is the
socialist perception of technology one which contests merely the
allocation of its products (its productivity, its wealth), assuming
that technology of itself is aloof from politics even while it impinges
on society?

What we are pointing to here is a tendency on the left to argue
that technology is the foundation on which socialism is to be
erected. Marx occasionally referred to this base as the 'realm of
necessity', considering – unproblematically – that until people had
adequate food, warmth and shelter there was no place for politics,
for everyone's energy was required to survive the strictures of
nature. This viewpoint unavoidably puts an unstated number of
elemental issues, much technology included, beyond politics. It is
best illustrated in the history of the Soviet Union where each
technological innovation was (and is) regarded as an expression of
socialist success[19] since the chief yardstick of advance was the speed
of industrialization. There is also a strong flavour of it in *The
Communist Manifesto* where capitalism's capacity to bring about
'the rapid improvement of all instruments of production'[20] is
admired as a means of building up the technological infrastructure
which the working class will eventually inherit and enjoy.[21]

This way of seeing consistently represents socialism as a system
which harnesses technology's productivity for *more* and for more
equitable distribution. At root it regards technology in much the
same way as Toffler and Martin: it is a means, indeed the privileged

means, of increasing efficiency and assuring an escape from scarcity. It must, therefore, be embraced in the name of reason itself. In this light, there is a politics of technology, but it is one which restricts itself to encouraging acceptance and indeed celebration of whatever wonders the latest 'Scientific Technological Revolution' might provide and limits itself to questions concerned with the allocation of technology's output. Crucially, it accepts that technology must impose itself on social and even political relations because it is the precondition of establishing any meaningful politics. Read in this way, much of the socialist tradition is quite as technologically determinist as that of futurist technoboosters.

The upshot is that faced, as now, with a period of intensive technological innovation, there is on the left a resigned feeling of the 'inevitability' of adoption of new technologies, though it is widely agreed that they exacerbate unemployment and bolster the power of the already powerful.[22] After all, how could one in conscience resist technologies if, fundamentally, they achieve greater productivity which would – 'if only we had a Labour government' – be used for the benefit of the poor rather than, as now, for abuse by the rich?

By the same token, there is resignation to the social relationships that these advanced technologies appear to force upon people. Thus the technologies of large-scale manufacture and bureaucratic administration are regarded as 'facts of life' that are determined by the imperative of maximizing output. The relations of authority and expertise which accompany these – and the consequent social and economic divisions between management, experts and operatives – are similarly deferred to as 'unavoidable' necessities.

Finally, socialists must feel acutely uncomfortable when they encounter the future projected by Toffler and his kind because so many of its aspirations are socialistic. Catch on to the big 'third wave', he says (as do his many acolytes in media, business and political circles, Dr David Owen, for example, considering that 'Alvin Toffler has more to offer the left today than Karl Marx'[23]), and ride effortlessly into a socially conscious, communal society where everyone belongs and no one goes without. To reach this nirvana, announces one-time Marxist Toffler, all one needs to do is accede to new technologies that promise wonderful communications that string together home, office and nation-states, as well as bringing material superabundance. We can make it, attests Christopher Evans, thanks to the 'mighty micro', and 'without the long-awaited revolution of the proletariat'. Why, claims Anthony Hyman, the magnificent generosity of the new technology is at last beginning to make it possible for society to move in the direction of its old dream, never realizable but a splendid goal, the dream that was appropriated by Marxism and then lost in the monolithic politics of the twentieth century: from each and all according to their inclination and ability; to each according to need.[24]

Socialists, long accepting that technology is necessary to provide the basis for socialism without stipulating either how much technology will be required or to what extent the technology will impose itself on social arrangements and thereby override politics, cannot really complain when conservatives steal their fire by discovering in new technology the possibility of 'socialism' without political upset or even change because it can take us effortlessly to the 'affluent redundancy' of an 'Athens without Slaves'.

For a politics of technology

What most socialists and futurists share is the conviction that technology is *prior* to politics insofar as it is the basis upon which political programmes are built. For this reason the futurists, encountering an array of computer communications technologies that have recently begun to come available, announce that these will carry us rapidly, and perhaps for some recalcitrant souls bumpily, into an 'information age' in which the major political debates will be concerned with how to spend massive periods of leisure and enjoy a surfeit of goods. Socialists agree that IT is set to change the world dramatically, and admit that we are entering a 'post-industrial' era, though their view is that it will be necessary to agitate politically over how best to share out this new society's wealth since this will decide whether we have 'post-industrial socialism' or 'post-industrial capitalism'.[25]

These approaches seem to us to ignore two major contributions of the greens to an understanding of the significance of technological change. This refusal to admit to green propositions may not be surprising on the part of futurists such as Toffler whose role in life was to speculate on the 'impact' of technology on society, but from the left it is disappointing and debilitating since it directly influences the capacity to comprehend the meaning of technological innovation and thereby weakens the effectiveness of radical political initiatives.

We take the value of the greens' contributions to be an insistence that technology cannot be adequately conceived as an abstraction, but rather must be considered concretely, and that technology, from its origination to its application, should be regarded in political terms. That is, greens argue that the concept 'technology', while it may be useful as a generic and shorthand expression, actually misleads when it comes down to questions of practical policies towards specific technologies. No one can be against 'technology' because 'technology', as such, does not exist.[26] Rather, an enormous variety of technologies is to be found in particular machines performing particular functions in the service of particular ends. If we can move towards that level of analysis, away from the unreal issue of 'are you for or against technology?' to a vigorous insistence on comprehension of the *contexts* of technological innovation, then we can begin to discriminate *this* technology from *that* one instead of being forced to endorse all 'technology' as inherently 'progressive'. Moreover, if we do that we can also start to see that technologies bear the imprint, in complex and often intricate ways to be sure – in design, development and implementation – of social relations, of power, values, priorities, interests and motives. And if we can do this we can sensibly begin to make *political* decisions about the desirability of encouraging *these* technologies rather than *those*. As regards understanding and acting on the 'information technology revolution', these principles have important consequences. Let us show why.

Information Technology and market imperatives

The UK is now wallowing in the worst economic depression of this century. It is this stark fact that above all else provides the rationale demanding the application of new technologies and investment in research and development (R&D). This sets the context and politics of technological innovation. A derivative of this is 're-structuring' followed by 'labour flexibility' and 'shake out'. An appropriate response has elicited a shift of educational emphasis towards 'relevance' as defined by those with the power to make *their* definitions stick. Accordingly educational institutions adopt the new technologies. In this way, so goes the argument, IT will improve our productivity whilst simultaneously improving the quality of our products and so help us win a larger share of the world's market for goods and services. The resulting prosperity will create more and better jobs in new industries as they replace the old.

This is the logic acceded to by all of the political parties. There are certainly differences of approach between Labour, which favours a state-led race to gain the lead in the IT challenge, and the Conservative Party, which puts its trust in the vitality of less directed private capital, but these tactical differences are secondary to acceptance of the rules of a pre-established game.

There is no secret about any of this. For example, it was James Callaghan who, as a Labour Prime Minister, pronounced that 1978 'has proved to be the year when Britain woke up to microelectronics' and urged the nation to meet head-on the 'challenge' of IT that we might strive successfully for its 'rewards'. If we do not quickly adopt it, he went on, 'and other major industrial countries adapt . . . then the prospect for us will be of stagnation and of decline'.[27] In the same way, Kenneth Baker, by 1981 the Minister for IT in a Conservative administration, stressed the 'enormous opportunities' IT held out for the country to regain its international stature so long as we were not 'left behind in this technological race'. He went on: 'We shall have to run very fast to keep ahead of the newly emerging countries [since] we cannot resist the trend of progress.'[28]

It is generally the case that the argument is couched in a language which has it that a technological discovery – 'the microelectronics revolution' – makes inevitable our readjustment to new circumstances. But a moment's reflection leads one to realize that we must adapt immediately not because of any technological breakthrough, but because of the consequences for our competitive position of not improving, or at the least stabilizing, our place in the market. Across the spectrum politicians shroud this brutal truth by announcing that 'the inevitable logic is that we must accept the technologies' (Kenneth Baker, Tory),[29] that 'the British people in all walks of life . . . must recognize that we have to accept the advent of the new technology' (John Evans, Labour),[30] that 'technological change will not be halted' (Shirley Williams, Social Democrat).[31] But behind this technocratic reasoning lies the pressing economic exigency: 'Automate or liquidate'.[32] If we do not rapidly accommodate the new technologies, the Japanese, Americans, West Germans, French . . . even the New Zealanders will, and thereby they will steal our markets, leaving us helpless to stop the slide down the league table of prosperous nations.

Still further behind this proposition is the assumption that while technological developments and the international market impose themselves on us, there is no cause for concern – other than that we must adjust post-haste if we are to benefit – since these are neutral phenomena. This is the position of Conservative, Labour and

Alliance parties alike: the concern of all is for distribution of the proceeds of technological innovation successfully introduced in the competitive race. For all three parties politics enters only at this later stage, at the point of the allocation of resources which come to us from adroit adjustment to IT (something which might require political intervention to smooth its way by timely subsidy, redirecting school curricula, and so on) and market demands.

But it is demonstrably the case that a technology policy guided by the principles of the market shapes the technologies that are produced and applied. As regards the microchip, though it is the case that fundamentals of computer science and electronic engineering were essential for its development, it is striking that economic and political circumstances were particularly conducive to its pioneering in 1960s America and that these conditions shaped the practical products (manufacturing plant, military technologies) in which integrated circuits were embodied.[33] At this time of boom in the US economy, with high tech companies boosted by defence contracts that were inflated by the Vietnam War, the priority of research and development programmes was to create technologies that the market deemed valuable. Because that was and is the major principle underlying the production of *this* technology rather than *that* one, an important consequence was that the finished goods bore the imprint of prospective clients. And it is the same today, though the market imperative is felt much more keenly in time of crisis. Because the overriding concern for producing and applying IT today is 'how can we best our competitors?', the outcome is that many jobs are routinized, simplified and deskilled[34] since these cheapen costs and aid increases in production. The starting point is the market rather than, let us say, how to ennoble work processes. Can anyone think of a single engineering project with a brief to improve the conditions of labour as opposed to getting more production for less expense? It is only to be expected therefore that the technologies that are developed will accord with this principle.

Again, if the market is the arbiter of technological success or failure, it is likely that it will impose itself on the technologies that are allowed to leave the drawing board. A startling example of this intrusion – startling because it was an overt expression of what must be a generally tacit reasoning – was given in 1980 by the chairman of Thorn-EMI when he announced that his company's 'decision to withdraw from medical electronics was [because] there appeared little likelihood of achieving profits in the foreseeable future'.[35] The Lucas Aerospace workers who devised an alternative plan for the production of socially useful rather than commercially attractive technologies illustrated the same process. The Lucas Aerospace Combine Committee's suggestions that the expertise of their members be put to the manufacture of medical equipment (portable kidney machines, sight substitution aids for the blind, artificial limb control systems, and so on), alternative energy technologies (solar-cell technology, a flexible power pack, and so on), road-rail vehicles and other technologies were not rejected by management because they were technically unfeasible. On the contrary, the company's retort had nothing to say about the viability of these ideas as technologies. Its considerations were singularly commercial when it announced that

> it intends to concentrate on its traditional business which involves the development of aircraft systems and components for the aerospace and defence industries [because] the only way to secure jobs in the market economy is to manufacture the products which the Company is best at producing efficiently and profitably.[36]

Information Technology and market power

Information Technology is much more than a technology: it is also a business, a global one that is dominated by a few privileged transnational corporations, the influence of which is felt on the diverse range of computer communications technologies now available and currently emerging. At the forefront of these corporate giants stands IBM (International Business Machines; 1984 revenue $45.9 billion) which dominates world computing, accounting for something like 80 per cent of the mainframe computer market and a major force in every other IT sector of significance.[37] Close behind IBM – some would say in tandem – is AT&T (American Telegraph and Telephone; 1984 revenue $33.2 billion), followed by a cluster of multi-billion dollar earners such as Digital Equipment, Nippon Electric Company, Siemens, Hitachi, ITT, and Honeywell.

These companies possess both the vast resources necessary to survive the fierce competition taking place in the IT market and, just as important, the financial clout to force or keep out usurpers.[38] They also have the funds to purchase strategically important wings of the business when it suits their purposes. Thus IBM could afford in 1985 to buy out MCI Communications, a telecommunications company earning $1.9 billion in 1984, while AT&T has bought 25 per cent of Olivetti (1984 earnings $2.9 billion), one of Europe's leading data processing operators (and owner of Acorn Computers in Britain), and has entered a co-operative deal with Philips of Holland to present a 'global challenge' to IBM's ambitions to be the major force in computer communications. The only serious new entrants to this industry are equally wealthy transnationals, vividly illustrative of which is General Motors (1984 revenue $83.8 billion) which took over Hughes Aircraft in the summer of 1985 for $5 billion,[39] a move that followed GM's payment of $2.5 billion for Electronic Data Systems the previous year. The conclusion of any description of the IT industry is inescapable: to get involved it is not enough to have a marvellous technological breakthrough because a requisite is to have available the million- (and billion-) dollar organizations that support sales outlets, research and development facilities, and a worldwide marketing network.

These corporate behemoths are involved in IT not for love of technological innovation, but because it appears a sound commercial investment. In pursuit of a goal which few of them attempt to hide (though often they present it in the nebulous terms of 'growth') – profit maximization – they tailor their strategies towards the production of the most marketable technologies. Broadly speaking, the richer the client the higher is the priority of the IT industry to meet his or her requirements. For that reason the concerns of the IT business are, in descending order: large corporate clients, the defence agencies and the general public (and within the latter the lion's share goes to 'entertainment', a minute portion to education).

The priority of market principles means that the likes of IBM targets the $8 billion it spent on R&D between 1977 and 1982 on creating technologies that have the most potential for profitable return, and not for creating technologies that will make the desert bloom. It is that, rather than any logic of technological progress, which results in the fact that the major computer communications systems are supplied to large corporate clients with massive and pressing informational needs, a large proportion of white-collar workers currently employed to handle and process this information, and an appetite for reducing the costs of these people and procedures. As the 'world leaders from broadcasting, teleommuni- cations, manufacturing and government' who met at Leeds Castle, Kent, in 1982 to discuss 'structural issues in global communications' concurred, these systems are developed to 'serve the intracorporate needs for which they were designed'.[40]

The relation between manufacturers of IT and their customers is symbiotic, the goal the same, and the effect on technologies palpable. Computer networks in and between national, international and intercontinental subsidiaries and headquarters have not resulted from the fortuitous 'discovery' of microelectronics. The critical factor in their manufacture and installation – that is, the critical factor in the creation of substantive technologies – is the desire of the producer to sell in the most lucrative markets and the buyer most effectively to reduce costs and secure control over the enterprise.

No one who is aware of the inexorable rise of the transnational corporation, dramatically so since 1945, and from the United States especially, can be unaware of the need of global companies to have sophisticated and reliable computer communications networks tying together their operations. The *Business Roundtable*, an organization certainly in the know since it represents leading sectors of American business, is candid:

> The dependence of multinational corporations . . . upon international information transfer is increasing. A 1983 survey, with 380 companies, from 85 countries participating, indicates that 94% of the corporations now use, or are planning to use, international computer-to-computer communications systems.[41]

A *Financial Times* report on Ford's 'global strategy' to manufacture a 'world truck' illuminates the same need. Ford's 'world truck' will

> have a European cab and panels shipped out from Europe as well as using the European name, Cargo. It will have a North American chassis, a diesel engine developed from one used by the group's agricultural tractor division. And it will be assembled in Brazil for the domestic and North American markets.[42]

These sorts of production processes, which are leading to the increasingly centralized control of deliberately diversified operations,[43] are unthinkable without modern computer communications technologies. And it is hard to imagine these technologies being devised or put into place without the need emanating from affluent transnational corporations.

Information Technology and political power

The development of computer communications systems to suit the requirements of an extensive transnational empire undoubtedly bolsters the power of participating corporations. The hardware and software of the data networks that string together their activities enable them to manage what AT&T describes as 'global markets for the movement and management of information'.[44] This puts them in an advantageous position compared to poor countries that cannot afford a similar informational infrastructure (how can the likes of Malawi and New Guinea afford their own satellites and computer systems?) and compared to workers located in isolated plants around the globe.

This is certainly not a narrowly economic issue. The interest of transnational capital in information networks has been a major factor shaping and sustaining the American political doctrine of the 'free flow of information'. An integrated global economy demands the movement of data and text across geographical boundaries between corporate locations. National interests or decisions should not be allowed to hinder it. However, over the last decade or so many nations have come to the conclusion that the 'free flow' policy, while (like technology) admirable as an abstract concept, in practice means freedom for the mighty, chiefly US, corporations to continue their domination of international trade. Moves have accordingly been made to establish a 'new world information order' that tries to redress the balance in favour of the poorer nations. At the United Nations and the United Nations Educational, Scientific and Cultural Organization (UNESCO) attempts have been made to reverse the present situation by, for example, limiting and/or insisting on scrutiny of the movement of economic, political and cultural information across national frontiers. The result has been sustained US pressure to retain the 'free flow' principle which has been of particular benefit to America. This is the pressure that culminated in US withdrawal from and ending financial support for UNESCO in 1984.[45]

There is a similar US enthusiasm for advocating a policy of the 'free market' in computer communications that stems from the fact that the manufacture of equipment and software is the monopoly of the rich nations. The predominance of IBM (Snow White) and Control Data, Honeywell, Digital Equipment, Sperry *et al* (the Seven Dwarfs) in computers is well known. Any of the other major technologies displays similar features. Typically, American corporations are world leaders, followed by Japanese conglomerates and a cluster of European electrical and electronic groups. It is in the interests of these to have open markets in which to compete because they start against any opposition (but their own internecine strife) with the enormous advantage of present dominance. Thus, for example, a US Department of Commerce report on telecommunications equipment observes that America accounted for $21.8 billion of a total world market of $45.6 billion in the early 1980s, with just two companies, AT&T's subsidiary Western Electric and ITT, notching up $17.03 billion of that, and the US, Japan and half a dozen European nations accounting for 90 per cent of world trade in such products.[46]

These dominant nations are prepared, even willing, to continue and even to increase their supply of IT to the rest of the world – *on condition that they subscribe to market precepts*. In the area of telecommunications a good many countries, including some of the rich nations themselves, have been perverse enough to establish nationally owned services that are answerable, in some way, to politicians who might favour purchase of equipment supplied by local industries, who often place conditions on orders that do not suit the commercial interests of foreign competitors, and who frequently insist that there are 'public service' clauses attached to the rules of operation of communications (for example, subsidy of 'uneconomic' services to remote rural areas by lucrative business thoroughfares).

Such presumptions threaten to diminish the ability of US corporations especially to continue and extend their dominance as suppliers of equipment and, increasingly, to develop their role as servicers of private communications networks such as the one that the General Motors subsidiary, Electronic Data Systems (EDS), wishes to supply to Unilever in the UK.[47] Recalcitrant nations are not to be tolerated, and in consequence American politicians – and it has been America, the biggest of the big, which has been most consistent in forwarding the *laissez-faire* policy in telecommunications, unlike Japan and western Europe where the free market has been willingly endorsed only outside particular national boundaries – have been called upon to act by the business lobby:

The future well-being of its [telecommunications'] supplier industries will depend critically upon their ability to perform in the international marketplace. At present foreign restrictions seriously constrain this essential type of growth and development.

It is imperative that the US government make full use of both bilateral channels and multilateral frameworks to minimize such interference, with the objective of affording American producers equitable opportunitites for competition and growth.[48]

The US government has awesome power at its disposal (foreign aid, trade embargoes, investment allocations, educational awards, and so on) to make any dissident nations fall into line. Britain and Japan have bowed to US pressure to 'liberalize' their telecommunications, though they have not completely accepted an open market in such a strategic indigenous industry. Other major nations are set to follow the same pattern. Third World countries will have considerably less power to resist American pressure.

The primacy of market principles helps ensure that already mighty US suppliers are advantaged, but it also affirms that IT networks will be designed with large corporate clients uppermost in mind, and this even when a particular telecommunications network is installed as a national system. Guy de Jonquieres describes why this might come about:

> some customers fear ISDN [Integrated Services Digital Network] may turn out to be over-elaborate, costly and designed mainly to suit the PTTs' (post, telegraph and telephone authorities) own engineers. They argue that the PTTs are still too far removed from commercial realities to cater adequately for the complex demands of modern businesses . . .
>
> 'Business users realize they are going to have to foot the bill for investments such as ISDN in the end. In return, they should have the right to get the services they need, not what PTTs think they ought to need,' says Mr George McKendrick, chairman of the International Telecommunications Users Group, which includes many large companies.[49]

What we have demonstrated here is the truism 'he who pays the piper calls the tune': economic and political muscle determine who gets what IT, for what purposes, in what circumstances, on what conditions, and in what form.

But to avoid misunderstanding, let us state bluntly that none of this detailing of the effects of context and politics on the process of technological innovation means, necessarily, that we are concluding that all particular forms of IT are unusable in different social circumstances. We live in the world, experiencing the weight of past and present legacies which bear on plans for the future, and we must start from what we have. It would be a crazy advocacy to suggest that, since present technologies are marked by previous social relationships, future social policy would do away with all existent technology. What this detailing should achieve, however, is the realization that any account which commences with the presupposition that there has been an 'IT revolution', the adoption of which is 'inevitable', and that we have straightforward 'choices' that will allow us to apply it for 'good' or 'bad' though at root it is a sign of 'progress', is misconceived. The only adequate way of understanding the import of these technologies is to see them as an integral part of social, economic and political processes. As part of the environment in which we all live.

Information Technology and the military

Paul Bracken has observed that nuclear weapons *qua* weapons of destruction reached 'maturation' during the 1960s. Today we have a lot more of them, but the weapons themselves have not changed dramatically. What has changed, however, is that modern nuclear 'defence' has developed in two important ways: there has been created the 'vertical integration' of warning and intelligence systems with actual weapons and the systems used in war, and dispersed military commands have undergone 'horizontal integration' into a single centralized structure of command.

The consequence of this is that the conduct of nuclear war is unimaginable without highly complex, fast-acting and, increasingly, automatic command, control, communications and intelligence (C3I) technologies. By the same token, prime targets nowadays for an enemy hoping to minimize its own losses in war are the C3I systems of its opponents. Because of this, never-ending efforts are made to make these still faster-acting, more reliable and durable.[50]

Moreover, while C3I for nuclear weapons is the most dramatic instance of the crucial role of computer communications in contemporary military affairs, IT finds application in virtually all areas of defence as 'electronic warfare' has become since the 1960s its defining characteristic.[51] Whether it is battlefield communications, radar-seeking weapons, Exocet missiles, electronic counter-measures and electronic counter-counter-measures, the militarization of space (some 80 per cent of satellites in orbit are for military purposes), AWACS (airborne warning and control systems) aircraft or the World-Wide Military Command and Control System

(Wimex) that ties together thirty military centres, the conduct of military matters without IT is scarcely possible.

The most dramatic example of IT's role in modern warfare is the American Strategic Defence Initiative (SDI or Star Wars). On it rides the greater part of the US effort to develop 'fifth-generation' computer communication systems which will be essential to co-ordinate observation of manifold enemy actions and locations and to manage the release and targeting of beam weapons. There are two reasons why this should be so. First, the Star Wars concept assumes that computers can be devised which can digest and act upon enormous quantities and qualities of information from many sources in a matter of seconds (that is, so that the launch of enemy missiles can be detected immediately and then the missiles destroyed before they get underway for their flight time of a very few minutes). Secondly, the sums of money pouring from the military sector are so huge that every major IT corporation in the USA has a large stake in obtaining a share.

The expenditure committed to SDI is gargantuan: up to $30 billion for use in the first five years of the project, with an estimated total many times that. Thousands upon thousands of researchers are employed in computing, engineering, electronics and cognate disciplines, all briefed to produce required technologies. While it is commonplace to claim that these military projects will have civilian benefits (the space programme is famous for having given to civil society the non-stick frying pan) there are two reasons at least why one might be sceptical. The first is that the director of the 'science and technology office' of the Pentagon's SDI programme, Dr James Ionson, says that the work will have to be 'mission oriented' (sic), aimed above all at producing technologies for an operational Star Wars system in the 1990s.[52] To be sure, there is no guarantee that the 'mission' will be successfully completed, just as there will, in all likelihood, be some by-product from the many million-dollar research programmes that may find alternative uses. But surely no one will contest that the SDI paymasters, in dictating the terms within which the research is to be conducted, enormously restrict the possibilities of creating technologies with non-military uses. The second reason for scepticism is the serious doubts already entertained as to whether wider society will be able to find uses for the super computers under consideration. Anthony Tucker poses the problem thus:

The driving force for machines of such immense capability in the US are the military requirements for simulation and real-time control of highly complex systems [but] as far as anyone knows the world civil market for machines of the scale envisaged will hardly run into double figures.

Tucker continues to note that Europe's answer to Star Wars, the much-vaunted Eureka programme championed by France, is being undertaken so that European computer communications industries can compete for C3I systems.[53] Lest that be considered a bad joke, we direct the reader's attention to news of a *Financial Times* conference, held in London on 4 and 5 November 1985, on the theme 'The SDI Eureka and Industry' which was advertised by the organizers as 'a forum to explain to international business executives the best prospects for them in the ... SDI programme and give guidance on how they can best position themselves to secure contracts'.[54] In addition, it ought to be remembered that the Thatcher government, initially lukewarm towards SDI, raised more than a little enthusiasm when the possibility of winning orders worth up to $2 billion was presented.

Finally, in case it is thought by some that such military pressures are a peculiarity of the Americans, it is worth noting that Britain's strategy to develop a new generation of 'expert' computer systems is deeply implicated in defence programmes. Thus *Computing* recently opened a report on the state's £350 million plan to match the efforts of the Japanese and Americans:

All of the major multimillion pound software projects which are funded under the Government's Alvey scheme have now become primarily vehicles for defence programming.[55]

How can this influence of the military on the development of advanced technologies be welcomed by those who oppose the abuse of technology? Surely it shows that the argument that technology possesses its own inherent, fundamentally progressive logic is a false one. Military systems surely cannot be regarded as anything but the outcome of identifiable social and political priorities which value defence/war above the production of technologies for peaceful purposes. Moreover, it is hard to see any socially desirable order in which these technologies might be put to worthwhile use. All that one can legitimately hope for is that there will come a day when they are redundant, mere reminders of an age which constructed technologies into which were embodied values of distrust, aggression and hatred.

In the here and now, however, they not only bolster the centralized command of military leaders, but also threaten civil liberties throughout the wider society. In a crisis situation such as the heightened international tension leading up to a nuclear exchange, it is hard to imagine any public accountability[56] of military strategists on whether to launch particular weapons, especially since surprise could be crucial should it be decided that a pre-emptive strike at the enemy's C3I network was necessary. The publication by Duncan Campbell of details of three Emergency Powers Bills and an agreement with the USA which transfer draconian powers to military, police and government officials[57] makes doubly clear that those responsible for making contingency plans intend there to be no democratic participation in time of severe crisis.

But even on a day-to-day basis it seems that concern for 'national security' leads to widespread surveillance of the citizenry. To some degree this is an extension of the work of 'spying' agencies which are an accompaniment of elaborate C3I systems, notably Britain's Government Communications Headquarters (GCHQ) and America's National Security Agency (NSA) which, according to David Burnham of the *New York Times*, possesses 'what are believed to be the largest and most advanced computers now available to any bureaucracy on earth'.[58] Though it is extraordinarily difficult to estimate the amount of internal surveillance undertaken by and on behalf of the military, available evidence suggests that a large number of people in Britain and America are 'watched' by intelligence services for signs of 'subversion', their telephones tapped or metered, electronic bugs planted in their homes and places of meeting, and their personal histories examined. At MI5's Mayfair headquarters a computer file is kept of 500,000 subversives.[59] It also has access to many more and often larger files held by police throughout the country.[60] In addition, it has a right to draw on private data banks – health records, tax returns, bank accounts, and so on – which enable it to put together a composite picture of anyone targeted in the name of 'national security'. Reports that trade unionists, radical political parties, student organizations and the like are monitored regularly come to public view as a result of leaks and enterprising journalists, though surely the most astonishing appeared in August 1985 with the *Observer*'s account of how *all* key BBC appointments and staff working in news and current affairs are vetted by MI5.[61] Such revelations are a measure of the extent to which the 'security state' must undermine democracy in the name of protecting it from the 'enemy'.

To question 'need'

The heading for this section purposely shows 'need' in quotation marks. This is because in the necessarily political arguments that take place over the allocation of always finite and therefore inadequate resources, three different concepts are often conflated. These are the concepts of wants, demands and needs. In doing so the concepts of absolute and relative deprivation are also conflated. The argument is, then, often confused as the participants talk past rather than to each other, using the word 'need' when one of the other two is the more appropriate. It is important to note therefore that in the argument presented here what is usually described as a need is in fact a socially generated want or demand.[62]

The principle that 'need' is a social rather than a natural creation leads us to ask which circumstances define it in our society. This allows us in turn to reflect upon the effect of these needs on the production and application of practical technologies. What we have described in previous sections of this chapter are particular 'needs' which have imposed themselves on the development and usage of IT: the 'needs' of an economy deep in recession, the 'needs' of a transnational corporate system, the 'needs' of a military-industrial complex. Herbert Schiller has forcefully posed the crucial issue that arises from this situation:

> It is by no means indisputable that what is required by and serviceable to the dominant groups in the privileged core of the world economic order, is necessary or acceptable in either the outlying regions, dependent on and exploited by the center, or in fact, for the general public in the center itself.[63]

If we raise the issue of need in this way, stressing that its defining characteristics in our society are who can afford to buy and what can be sold, then a great deal of the 'inevitability' of adjusting to the 'progress' of the 'IT revolution' is cast into doubt – and with it the utopias of the futurists and the socialist conviction that technology is inherently beneficial.

But we can go much further than that. Thinking about the social conditions which give rise to conceptions of need leads one to realize that a key feature of capitalism is that needs are deemed to be insatiable. If 'needs' were natural, they would also be finite, as true needs are, but the possibility of reaching a stage of development when all 'needs' were fulfilled would risk bringing to a halt the dynamic of our economy. Because the health of the economy rests on the presumption that the market will constantly stimulate suppliers (and if it did not there would be permanent crisis), it is paradoxical that the world's wealthiest societies 'dedicate themselves to the proposition of scarcity'[64] and go to great lengths to ensure that 'needs' are never fully satisfied.

Very many people gain their livelihoods in organizations whose purpose is to try to persuade the public that there is a need for the objects and services their clients are marketing. Advertising is the obvious example of this creation of 'need' and, thinking of the hype used to convince anxious parents that if their children do not have an Apple or Sinclair personal computer they will be educationally and employably disadvantaged, we would not want to underestimate its importance.[65] What should be stressed is that the production of desire is not something that simply follows the manufacture of a given product. It is rather that our whole economy revolves around the concept of marketing, around the idea that selling is the be-all and end-all of life.[66] This value intrudes into media campaigns, the packaging of goods, their display in shopping arcades, the regular redesign of products, and into the process of technological innovation itself.

We may relate this to the consumer capitalism in which we find ourselves. As the economy has become more and more reliant on the sale of goods and services (automobiles, electrical/electronic goods, entertainment, and so on) to individuals,* so there have developed a number of characteristics which distinguish our society. Two in particular should be emphasized. One is the individualistic outlook and accountancy which consumerism, with its ability-to-pay yardstick, stimulates. Along with this goes the notion that need is a matter of personal disposition, to be answered by purchases that will be used privately. It is made manifest in a hedonistic mentality that corresponds with a withdrawal into a home-centred existence which is more and more elaborately

---

*There have of course long been consumer goods, but in the distant past economic activity was primarily agricultural and, in the nineteenth century, a large part of industry was devoted to supplying goods to railways, shipping, iron and steel and similar concerns, rather than to individuals.

equipped with electronic aids and diversions (for those with the wherewithal to buy them). This drive towards the privatization of life is still resisted and by no means complete, but its direction is clear and its advance palpable. A cognate feature of this trend is an unwillingness to see need either in social terms or as amenable to resolution by collective measures.[67]

A second characteristic is that, as corporate capital has grown throughout this century, it has diligently sought to improve its control over its operations. For the obvious reason that irregularity of consumption jeopardizes smooth production, the history of corporate expansion has been one of a search to market most effectively.[68] A crucial dimension of this has been a determination to build on past successes in the manufacture of new – and constantly renewed – goods and services. As regards consumer goods, it has meant in recent years that almost all of them have been produced as forms of enhanced television – hence cable, direct-broadcast satellite, video disc and cassette, TV games, and so on are the preponderance of IT for the 'general public', and with them goes a content which is overwhelmingly 'entertainment' orientated,[69] and encourages a stay-at-home lifestyle.

We would not want to argue either that corporate capitalism has been uniformly successful in its endeavours or that the enhanced television it presents to the consumer cannot be put to alternative uses,[70] but we do want to suggest that these particular technologies cannot be seen as answering, straightforwardly, unmet 'needs' of the public, because the 'needs' of the market economy have been primary considerations in their development. Against these criteria, we would put the greens' maxims: Do we really need these things? Who says that we need them and why do they say it? What sort of needs would we prefer to have satisfied by what sort of technology?

Conclusion

A requisite of gaining control over our lives and hence over our environment is that we see things as they really are. The premise of this chapter is that the approach of many socialists and futurists misconceives technological change and that the greens' insistence that we place questions of context and politics at the centre of technological change is essential to understanding its substance and significance.[71] If we can do that, we can begin to demystify something which always seems to have arrived from out of the blue to change us irrevocably. Moreover, in placing on the agenda the greens' questions – 'whose needs, who defines them, using what criteria?' – we can open up a series of issues far more radical than the socialist programme of redistribution. For as the IT juggernaut rolls on and over us, those issues urgently need raising.

4. Redefining the Environmental 'Crisis' in the South

Michael Redclift

There are three essential steps in explaining the nature of the environmental 'crisis' in the South:

1 We need to re-examine what we mean by the 'environment' in the context of developing countries.

2 We need to be clearer about the relationship between environmental problems in developing countries and the role of developed countries in their creation.

3 We need to re-examine the methods that are used for planning or 'managing' the environment in developing countries.

Particularly since the Stockholm Conference in 1972 there has been increased world interest in the environmental problems of developing countries. Reports like the *World Conservation Strategy* (1980) and collaborative research like UNESCO's *Man and the Biosphere* (MAB) programme have drawn attention to the gravity of the situation in the South. We are much better informed than we were about the symptoms of ecological degradation following the extensive documentation of the 'eco-crisis' in Less Developed Countries (LDCs).[1] In addition, attempts to 'model' the outcomes of this degradation have increased in sophistication.[2] Public attention has been drawn to the 'ecological crisis' through the media of television, video and print journalism. Non-governmental agencies like Oxfam and War on Want have emphasized in their development work the role of sustainable resource uses as a solution to environmental problems. Not least, government and inter-government agencies have been created to tackle these problems. The number of countries with government departments dealing with environmental management has grown from fifteen in 1972 to 115 in 1980.[3]

There is, then, no lack of attention to the Third World's environmental problems. Why do they remain and, in most cases, continue to assume greater proportions? The answer to this question lies partly in the *way* environmental problems are identified and partly in the *means* that are required to deal effectively with them. Redefining the environmental crisis in the South is a first step towards effective action – whether on the part of political organizations, voluntary bodies in the developed countries, governments or international agencies. Before considering these questions in detail it is worth considering whether they have historical roots.

Tenochtitlan and Mexico City – development and European colonialism

Compare the following accounts of the same place, the Valley of Mexico, one of which describes the situation there in 1984, the other the situation some 470 years earlier.

Valley of Mexico (1984)
The following description of the Valley of Mexico, provided by the Office for Urban Development and Ecology of the Mexican government, formed part of its submission to the *Man and the Biosphere* programme of the United Nations.[4]

The Valley of Mexico is located in the extreme south of the central *mesas* and covers a surface area of 9,600 square km. The land is suitable for crops, fruits, natural pastures and man-made grasslands. The main land use problems are linked to the lack of soil nutrients, erosion, salinity, alkalinity and flooding. Overgrazing and excessive deforestation have led to extensive resource depletion in the valley.

[There are also] serious pollution problems, due as much to the wastes resulting from domestic daily activities as to wastes from large industrial zones. Pollutants are emitted from industry, motor vehicles (2 million cars) and 'natural' dust storms which originate in the areas around the dried-up Lake Texcoco in the N.E. of the city and which blow human waste from these sewage outlets all over the Federal District.

Waste disposal is a major problem. The metropolitan area produces 6,000 tons of solid waste each *day*, of which only 75% is collected. The rest is scattered throughout the city, most of it on open untreated dumps. Those in 'marginal' settlements near the dumping grounds are most severely affected by these wastes and there is resulting environmental degradation, through methane production, and through soil and water contamination.

The population, currently about seventeen million, is expected to reach about thirty million by the year 2000. Today water is transported long distances across mountainous regions to the Federal District. Electrical consumption for pumping water may well double between 1985-8 and then *double again* by 1990 if the waters from the Tecolutla Basin have to be raised about 2,000m over a distance of 200 km. At present 50% of the land surface is affected by problems of erosion. If deforestation, overgrazing and inappropriate agricultural practices continue as at present, an even more critical situation will result. The problem is compounded by continued urban incursion into highly productive agricultural land which results in a lowering of agricultural production.

Valley of Mexico (1519)
The following extracts are from Bernal Diaz's account, four and a half centuries earlier.[5]

During the morning [8 November 1519], we arrived at a broad causeway and continued our march towards Iztapalapa, and when we saw so many cities and villages built in the water and other great towns on dry land and that straight and level causeway going towards Mexico, we were amazed and said that it was like the enchantments they tell of in the legend of Amadis, on account of the great towers and cues and buildings rising from the water, and all built of masonry. And some of our soldiers asked whether the things that we saw were not a dream ... With such wonderful sights to gaze on we did not know what to say, or if this was real that we saw before our eyes . . . [With Montezuma], we went to the orchard and garden, which was a marvellous place both to see and work in. I was never tired of noticing the diversity of trees and the various scents given off by each, and the paths choked with roses and other flowers, and the many local fruit trees and rose bushes, and the pond of fresh water . . . We must not forget the gardens with their many varieties of flowers and sweet-scented trees planted in order, and their ponds and tanks of fresh water into which a stream flowed at one end and out of which it flowed at the other, and the baths that [Montezuma] had there, and the variety of small birds that nested in the branches, and the medicinal and useful herbs that grew there ... I may add that on all the roads they have shelters made of reeds or straw or grass so that they can retire when they wish to do so, and purge their bowels unseen by passers by, and also in order that their excrement shall not be lost . . .

We saw the three causeways that led into Mexico . . . We saw the fresh water which came from Chapultepec to supply the city, and the bridges that were constructed at intervals on the causeways so that the water could flow in and out from one part of the lake to another. We saw a great number of canoes, some coming with provisions and others returning with cargo and merchandise; and we saw that one could not pass from one house to another of that great city and the other cities that were built on the water except over wooden drawbridges or by canoe . . .

The city which the Conquistadores discovered in the Valley of Mexico on 8 November 1519 was a remarkable 'island capital' which covered over twenty square miles. The combined population of Tenochtitlan and Tlatelolco was between 200,000 and 300,000, five times the size of Henry VIII's London. Indeed the population of Mexico as a whole was probably in the region of eleven million, many times that of England.

What surprised and fascinated Bernal Diaz most was the 'agricultural' nature of the city he discovered. It was divided, on a grid system, by long canals intersected by river 'streets'. Between these 'streets' were rectangular plots of land with houses built on them. These were the *chinampas*, the raised vegetable beds which provided most of the produce consumed in the city. These raised beds had been known to the lowland Maya during their 'Classic' period – as long ago for the Aztec population of Tenochtitlan as their civilization is to us. Constructing canals from the thick marsh vegetation, the Aztec people had piled up the surface vegetation like green 'mats'. Then, from the bottom of the canals, they had used mud to spread over the green 'rafts', which were anchored by planting willows all round them. The fertile plots that were constructed in this way produced a variety of crops, vegetables and fruit trees. Houses were built of light cane and thatch and, on drier ground, even of stone and mortar.

This enterprise met with problems which had to be overcome. Communication was by way of planks laid over the canals. To reduce salinization of the water supplies – the lake was high in salt content – a ten-mile dyke was constructed, sealing off a spring-fed freshwater lagoon for Tenochtitlan. Through human ingenuity the Aztecs were able to turn ecological obstacles to their advantage.

The *chinampas* were also extremely productive. As late as 1900 they still supplied some vegetables to Mexico City from the much reduced Xochimilco beds, all that remained of the *chinampa* capital. Three harvests were possible, with transplanting from reedbeds; animals were kept and their manure (together with that of humans) used on the organic gardens. In recent years there has been a growth of interest in raised-bed systems in Mexico and elsewhere.[6]

Our interest in *chinampas*, however, need not be confined to their current agronomic potential, important as that is. The accounts of pre-Columbian sustainable agriculture should also lead us to more fundamental questions about 'development' itself, and the role of the environment in the development process. Should we dignify with the term 'development' a process which leads millions of people to sacrifice their health and energies to survival? Perhaps an ecological alternative lies not so much in learning things we do not know as in 'unlearning' things we do know?

Within fifty years of Bernal Diaz's arrival, the cities of Tenochtitlan/Tlatelolco were pale shadows of their former selves. The pre-Columbian hydraulic system, analogous in the New World to the systems that had raised the ancient civilizations of China and the East,[7] had been irrevocably destroyed. The delicate ecosystems that had once supported millions of people on a sustainable basis were in ruins. The first post-Conquest agricultural production crises in Mexico, especially in 1538 and 1543, were what we would term 'resource crises' today. The attempts to utilize the water from the lake complex for irrigating new land and for flood prevention were ill judged and largely unsuccessful. At the same time the urban population grew throughout the colonial period, a population which could only be fed by 'tribute' collected from indigenous communities whose environment, like their culture, bore the brunt of colonial exactions.[8]

By the eighteenth century the establishment of the *hacienda* or large estate, together with the use of plough and animal traction, enabled the Valley of Mexico to achieve self-sufficiency in agricultural production. Most of the indigenous population, however, was deprived of land and pushed into increasingly marginal areas where it reverted to subsistence production. The need to clear much of the land of forest, together with the insatiable demand for wood from Mexico City (which required 25,000 new trees a year during the late colonial period), meant that deforestation was severe in the valley. Both indigenous communities and *haciendas* played a part in this decline.[9]

Changes in land use have been even more dramatic during this century. The *hacienda* system established under colonial rule was largely replaced in the post-revolutionary period by a combination of *ejidos* and peasant communities.[10] In a sense this marked a return to greater self-provisioning in agriculture. However, the urban growth of Mexico City dictated a quite different pattern of resource use from that established in pre-Columbian times. Food supplies for the urban economy came from further afield and the immediate environment became important for the provision of two other commodities: land and labour. The need for cash income, with which to enter into exchange relations, ensured that 'peasant' agriculture in the Valley of Mexico existed in name only. Most of the population in the peri-urban area, and much of the land, became incorporated in the increasingly centralized and specialized growth of Mexico City. In the space of four centuries an environment built on sustainable agriculture (*chinampas* and terrace cultivation) had been replaced by one in which labour and land became first separated and then recombined (the *hacienda/* community) under a new technology (plough and animal traction). The objective, to ensure control over the economic surplus, was achieved at the cost of destroying the indigenous ecological and cultural systems. Finally, the redistributive changes ushered in by the Mexican Revolution of 1910 provided a means to 'modernization', whose ultimate effect was to increase social inequality and place the local ecology in jeopardy. Mexico City became the material representation of a new kind of 'development', in which economic growth assumed more importance than either the satisfaction of basic human needs or the pursuit of complementary ecological and social systems.

The social construction of the environment

The extended discussion of one case, the Valley of Mexico, enables us to make some general observations about the role of the environment in the development process.

First, when we refer to 'the environment' in developing countries we are referring to something which has been produced by history, through struggles and exploitation, usually as part of the colonial and post-colonial accumulation process. Only when we refer to 'natural' wilderness is the colonial imprint relatively unimportant – and wilderness areas, especially in the humid tropics, are increasingly penetrated by metropolitan capital today. It is important not to divorce the environment from its parts, especially the human populations whose productive activities have contributed to its evolution.

Second, most pre-capitalist small-scale societies depend upon good ecological management to ensure future production. For hunters and gatherers, slash-and-burn cultivation and most 'peasant' or pastoralist groups, the viability of the 'natural' environment is a condition of their existence. There is no divorce between their 'culture' and their ecology; 'nature' as a social category assumes importance in their very cosmology, their 'world view'. Their ecological practices are their cultural practices.

Third, the impact of capitalism in peripheral 'less developed' countries implies contradictions for those with limited access to resources and power. On the one hand the 'development' process brings them closer to the market, encourages the production of commodities and the sale of their labour for cash. On the other hand survival on any other terms becomes precarious. Self-sufficiency in food production or energy is difficult when labour, expecially that of women, has to be allocated to gaining cash or to meeting the exigencies of the market and the state. Under these circumstances poor people inevitably have greater recourse to their 'natural' environment – which acts as the focus of the household's attempt to reconcile the needs of the family with those of the market. Sometimes the only avenue of escape is migration – to the cities or 'across the border'. At other times no such safety valve exists, and ecological degradation ensues, as we have seen in the Sahel and Ethiopia. Where the natural resource base permits it, as in tropical 'frontier' areas such as the Amazon, households struggle with their environment, wresting control from 'nature' and assuming a critical role in the process of gradual land concentration. Class struggles exist, but they are mediated by the environment. As those who accumulate wealth dispossess others, they are relocated to 'new' frontiers or return to work as wage-labourers within export-orientated, capitalist production. In relatively rare instances social struggles are undertaken in defence of the 'natural' environment, as in the Chipko movement in India, where Hindu people adopted tree conservation as a last-ditch attempt to forestall external threats to their woodlands.

Underdevelopment and the environment

The picture is often a confused one, and environmentally minded individuals are unlikely to find in Third World situations an unequivocal commitment to environmental goals. Most of those who are blamed for causing ecological problems, especially the rural poor, are inarticulate and powerless. They seldom have the support of middle-class activists or a media committed to publicizing their case. Conservationists frequently regard them with disfavour, as a threat to other species and to their habitat. A holistic concern with what impoverishes environments reveals the role played by international capital, trade relations and high technology agriculture. But this concern meets with ideological objections from most wealthy people in developing countries, who have a considerable stake in the development process. In addition, ecological problems suffer from 'reductionism': if we seek explanations at a sufficiently local, 'micro' level, it *is* the rural poor who often destroy 'nature'.

In most cases the poor are not only blamed for ecological degradation but they are the losers by it. People are brought into opposition with their own environments in attempts to meet household necessities or finance deficit budgets. Those who control better land resources make greater use of chemical inputs and mechanical traction. The struggle for livelihood – which characterizes most interaction with the 'natural' environment in developing countries – becomes increasingly dependent on inappropriate technological 'fixes'. As ecological degradation proceeds, through deforestation, desertification or the salinization of irrigation systems, indigenous knowledge is lost. It becomes more difficult to see the relevance of practices designed to ensure sustainable future production when the agricultural credit bank is leaning heavily on you today. In extreme cases, where the environment offers no hope of a solution, indigenous knowledge is simply irrelevant. This is the case in many areas of Africa where pastoralism has declined in the face of the combined effects of governmental antipathy, urban policy bias, export cash cropping and severe drought. It is not the effect of economic, structural policies alone which accounts for the human casualties of ecological degradation, but it is not 'natural' disasters either. It is a potent combination of structural and environmental factors.

International dimensions

The environmental problems of developing countries are clearly linked to their insertion within the international economy. It is important to remember, however, that this insertion has an historical dimension and that we cannot reduce the problem of specific geographical environments to contemporary economic and political relations alone. We also need to understand the objectives of developing countries, and their ruling elites, as well as the way in which pursuing these objectives meets obstacles – and encouragement – from the international economic community, especially the industrial states making up the Organization for Economic Cooperation and Development (OECD).

Most developing countries in the South are interested in securing some sort of industrial base, at the very minimum one which would assist the development of their rural sectors. However, the level of industrialization achieved in North America, Europe and Japan lies outside the reach of countries in the South, even those in Latin America which partially industrialized during and after the Second World War. Two immediate issues need to be considered: are Less Developed Countries *allowed* to develop in the way they would like, given the interest of the developed countries in securing cheap raw materials and foodstuffs from the South? Also, do the resources exist in LDCs for a 'development' process which emulates, or replicates, the 'successful' development of the North?

Both these questions have clear implications for those interested in a political economy of the environment. It has proved impossible to shift the balance of advantage in trading relations or investment from the countries of the North to those of the South via the United Nations Commission on Trade and Development (UNCTAD) and similar multilateral agreements. Even the Brandt Report, which proposed modest reforms in North–South economic relations, met with few practical responses from the developed countries. As long as most LDCs remain poor and, in many cases, heavily indebted to the North, their development efforts will inevitably take a heavy toll of long-term ecological factors in the quest for short-term economic 'benefits'. Cash crops will continue to be grown for the developed country markets; cattle will be reared extensively, often on land with rich arable potential; insecticides will be used without proper precautions; industrial pollution controls will be almost nonexistent. Countries like Nicaragua that can ill afford to ship a valuable resource like cotton in an unprocessed form will continue to be forced to do so. In an analogous structural situation, that of Guatemala, it has been estimated that of the US $40,000,000 per year earned from cotton exports, about three-quarters left the country in the form of pesticides, spray planes, tractors, and so on, used as 'inputs' for growing cotton in a capital-intensive way. The *net* income for Guatemala from cotton exports was therefore only a quarter of what it appears to have been.[11]

If we assumed a different role for Guatemala in the international division of labour, cotton, instead of being sold raw, would be processed into thread, converted to cloth and made into shirts and other clothes. These would then be sold on the international market, creating domestic employment in the process. If we then asked 'how much land devoted to cotton would be needed to earn the same amount of foreign exchange?' the answer would be . . . rather less than one per cent of the land actually devoted to it! This case, which illustrates the structural constraints under which LDCs use their natural resources, also points to the close relationship between international economic relations and domestic land use and employment. The resources *do* exist for a more integrated form of development within many of the countries of the South, but they imply radically different trading and investment relations with the countries of the North.

It is still necessary to ask whether 'limits to growth' exist, but important to emphasize that these limits have a great deal to do with existing North-South economic relations. Demographic pressures on land and water resources exist in many LDCs, of course, propelling many of them to the edge of ecocatastrophe. But these pressures make sense only within the framework of international capitalism, in which poor countries provide supplies of raw materials and labour at market prices clearly beneficial to the rich. These global distributive issues are central to an understanding of every facet of the environmental problem – water supplies, soil erosion, food security, energy production and technological transfer.

Another aspect of the international situation which needs to be considered in the role of international organizations is the elaboration and implementation of environmental policy. There are a number of international organizations with a specifically 'environmental' brief. These include the International Union for the Conservation of Nature and Natural Resources (IUCN), founded in 1948; the World Wildlife Fund, formed in 1961; organizations of the Council of Europe with responsibilities towards the 'environment', and the United Nations Environment Programme (UNEP), formed after the Stockholm Conference in 1972. Most international organizations have a research or, at best, an advisory role in international 'environmental' policy. UNEP, for example, has the role of 'environmental' monitoring, 'environmental' planning and the dissemination of information. Its role has always been widely misunderstood, however. It is not a UN *executive* agency, empowered to carry out its own programmes in the member states (like FAO or UNESCO). Nor is it a sprawling UN organization with a huge professional staff and a correspondingly large budget. Most importantly, UNEP is not responsible for most of the world's 'natural' environment, most of which lies within the boundaries of sovereign nations which stand for no interference from UN bodies in their internal affairs.[12] The role of UNEP is to be a catalyst within the corridors of international opinion, raising consciousness of 'environmental issues' especially within the UN 'system'.

The reality is that UNEP has little money and few staff, even fewer incentives to offer and no means of enforcing its wishes. It is a little like creating the UK's Natural Environment Research Council (NERC) without pooling the financial resources of its constituent member organizations and without co-ordinating their management structure.[13] Even the official document which was produced as Britain's contribution to the debate initiated by the World Conservation Strategy had this to say about UNEP:

> At the end of the day, the unavoidable truth is that the combined resources of the governments who came together at Stockholm to create the UN Environment Programme have simply not:
>
> (a) funded the Programme adequately;
> (b) co-operated with it adequately;
> (c) intervened with sufficient vigour to improve its performance;
> (d) taken much notice of it (as governments) except when it suited their short-term ends.[14]

Technology and environmental control

In the last decade or so the view has often been expressed that the logic of environmental politics lies primarily in planning. The following is a representative example of this position:

> No goal is more central to the environmental movement or more politically contentious than comprehensive environmental planning. If one looks upon current environmental policy struggles for a sign or portent of the future direction of environmental politics, the quest for planning appears constantly . . . as a common objective.[15]

The author of this book goes on to cite four 'fears' that LDCs have about the transfer of environmental planning from the North to the South. These are: the fear of 'neoprotectionism', the fear that attention to ecology might divert foreign aid funds, the fear of environmental chauvinism in the conditions that need to be satisfied to receive aid, and fear of the cost of non-polluting technologies. These fears certainly exist, and they reflect the enormous difficulty in reconciling even modest development aspirations with global conservation goals and environmental management within LDCs. However, an even greater threat is represented by international agencies in the development field which act in concert with transnational corporations and governments to undermine ecological sustainability in the South.

One example is the Industry Co-operative Programme (ICP), a group of over 100 multinational agribusinesses that were housed in the FAO in Rome until 1978 and influenced FAO policies in favour of their private interests. Their objective was to make agricultural development more dependent on inputs such as 'improved' seeds, agricultural machinery and agrochemicals. These inputs are sold and patented by these same companies.[16] Although the ICP was finally thrown out of FAO under the pressure of public exposure from writers like Susan George and the late Professor Eric Jacoby, corporate influence continues to be brought to bear on international agencies, most notably the United Nations Development Programme (UNDP).

Changes in agricultural technology, especially the development of chemical and biotechnology, have enormous implications for LDC environments. Chemical-energy inputs are more divisible and less 'lumpy' than mechanical technologies and, in the form of new high yielding varieties of rice and wheat, played an important part in the 'green revolution' of the 1960s and 1970s. They are also operated from outside the farms and sold in 'packages'. The interest of large-scale capital lies in both selling the package and transforming the product. It is at the stage at which the product is transformed that most profit is made, when the 'value added' to raw food production is included. In the countries of the European Economic Community (EEC), the price currently paid by consumers for food is on average three times that paid to the farmers. One should not forget, either, that the price paid to the farmers in the EEC countries is heavily subsidized!

Recent changes in the agro-industrial complexes of the North suggest several trends with consequences for LDC environments.

First, the role of labour in agriculture will in the future be increasingly dictated by technological developments in the industrial sector. Biotechnology, for example, has been developed by venture capital but has already outgrown this stage of its development. Already, agrochemical firms are buying their way into biotechnology, partly as a result of growing concentration in the agrochemical sectors.[17] These firms have merged with, or acquired, seed companies, the large, diversified 'deep pocket' transnational corporations that are well established in the seed industry supplying the South. The oil, chemical and pharmaceutical industries need to expand into seeds if they are to translate biotechnological potential into commercial success. The solution is to sell the farmer seeds which have their own built-in, bio-engineered performance and need to be monitored and controlled from outside.

The role of the agro-industrial complexes in the North is important to developing countries in a number of ways, not least in their impact on the environment. Decision-making increasingly rests with people other than the farmer, while the poor farmer's lack of access to new technology may marginalize him further. By 'controlling' the 'natural' environment in which agricultural production takes place, new technologies offer the possibility of transforming natural resources. This technical process rests, in fact, on the concentration of capital and technology in the hands of fewer people. The external effects, in surrounding areas through water and soil pollution, are often carried far afield. In some cases there is an observable loss in the diversity of local species and in ecological sustainability.

The effects of these technological developments on LDC environments vary considerably. The lack of 'fit' between ecological systems and the technologies being introduced into the humid tropical areas of the South is discussed by Norgaard (1984).[18] He lists four main characteristics of the Amazon ecosystem: enormous species diversity, a highly specialized system of nutrient recycling, uncertain succession responses in the biomass and rapid rates of growth of the biomass. Given these characteristics a compatible social system would be one with the following characteristics. First, it would need to be a social system producing a variety of products for the regional market, often at a near-subsistence level. Second, it should involve the participation of native people using indigenous knowledge. Third, the social system should utilize technologies that were evolved in the tropics. Fourth, there should be the opportunity for formal and informal risk sharing. Lastly, decision-making power should rest with the people managing the ecosystem.

What has happened in the Brazilian Amazon bears little relationship to this. Attempts have been made to introduce technological changes which enable more crops to be grown for distant markets and more labour to be transplanted from areas such as the poor north-east of Brazil. These technologies were developed in the temperate zone, not in the tropics. Finally, decision-making power usually rests not with local people in command of their environments but with government bureaucracies and large corporations in Brazil's developed region, the centre-south, and with the developed countries. The social system that corresponds to the technological 'implants' is essentially incompatible with the ecology of the area.

The results are not difficult to predict, and can be observed in other similar humid tropical areas.[19] The transnational corporations leave when the development subsidies have run out and the soils have been depleted. The peasant farmers revert to a multi-cropping farming system, providing food crops for personal consumption and a way of spreading risks. Such a system resembles slash-and-burn agriculture which, combined with hunting and gathering, is precisely the pattern of farming developed by the original, indigenous population of the tropical forests to ensure a resumption in the fertility levels of the vulnerable soils and to provide time for a regrowth of the biomass. For such indigenous people ecological sustainability is a condition of agricultural production rather than an alternative to it. Finally, the social cost in the degeneration of the colonizers' communities should be considered as part of the environmental cost of this type of 'development'. Despite the heavy cost of expensive infrastructure in areas of tropical expansion, most of the population remains vulnerable to disease and has little access to social services or regular employment. Once again forms of 'development' have been promoted without attention to even middle-term environmental and social effects.

Environmental managerialism

The problems which an LDC faces in trying to develop a sustainable environment are not confined to transnational corporations and domestic elites. Transnational corporations can sometimes be 'kept out', perhaps through multinational action by LDCs organized for the purpose. Ruling classes are themselves 'dependent' on the economic relationships that obtain with the developed countries; if these relations are radically changed it will unsettle domestic elites as well. The third obstacle in the way of 'ecodeve-lopment' is in some ways more intractable, and concerns the way environmental planning and management have evolved from developed country experience.

Consider the three main objectives of the World Conservation Strategy (1980). They were:

(i)   the maintenance of essential ecological processes;
(ii) the preservation of genetic diversity, and
(iii) sustainable utilization.

Although these are eminently 'ecological' objectives, which raise few objections from advocates of different theoretical positions on development, the implications of trying to achieve them are more radical than is usually admitted. Outside the framework of the 'biosphere reserve', an area of land which is protected because of its 'environmental' quality, achieving each of the three objectives requires concerted political action of a type not commonly found. In the face of the combined effect of accelerating demographic growth, increasing market penetration and urban 'bias', an 'ecodevelopment' orientation implies redirecting the development process in rural areas of LDCs. How far does current intervention designed to achieve environmental objectives – what I shall term 'environmental managerialism' – provide a workable alternative to progressive ecological degradation?

There are various components of environmental management as practised in the South today. Most of them have been distilled from developed country experiences of conservation and planning, experiences which relate to industrial and 'post-industrial' societies rather than underdeveloped countries. For example, the problems of environmental conservation in developed countries are bound up with food surpluses rather than food deficits, hence environmental planning is more closely related to the management of agricultural contraction than to rapid agricultural growth. The value of amenity uses and aesthetic considerations looms large in the environmental movements of developed countries while they scarcely figure among the priorities of people in the South.

The central tenet of environmental assessment is that there is an optimum balance of natural resource uses, which can combine sustainability in agriculture, forestry and other activities such as recreation. To establish the ecological interests which need to be considered it is necessary to undertake an evaluation of resource potential. Land use planning is a key technique in this approach, but land capability is not considered alone. Procedures have been developed for cataloguing lists of species, conducting soil surveys and establishing conservation priorities. Planning controls are then used on 'designated areas', to ensure that activities in these areas conform with overarching conservation and planning objectives.

The armoury of environmental management has been augmented in recent years by the inclusion of methods for social and economic appraisal. The projected cost of 'environmental' losses can be assessed over an extended period, subject to the need to maintain an agreed level of ecological diversity. The emphasis in using cost/benefit analysis, environmental impact assessment and other socio-economic planning 'tools' is very much on measurability and quantification. As in the sphere of technological appraisal in the natural sciences, it is *techniques* which are evaluated not policies, still less their implementation. Just as the underlying assumption of environmental assessment is that there is an optimum 'balance' of resource uses, the underlying assumption of environmental management is that long-term political interests in the 'environment' are convergent. Sustainable development – unlike almost any other sphere of human activity – can be achieved through seeking consensus rather than conflict.

There are a number of objections to environmental managerialism as set out above. First, the 'environment' is usually considered only *after* the 'development objectives' have been set. The 'environmental' aspects of a development situation are thus separated from the other aspects, often including economic and social factors. Furthermore, since very few projects undertaken in LDCs are *primarily* 'environmental' in scope, 'development' objectives completely obscure any other objectives. For example, in the 1970s only in 8 per cent of World Bank supported projects were 'environmental' factors considered sufficiently serious to require the use of outside consultants.[20] In the majority of cases the costs of employing environmental assessment were less than 5 per cent of the total project cost.

There are wider implications of environmental managerialism as well. We are accustomed to regard access to the 'environment' ('countryside' in the UK) as a means of escaping from social control, whether it is friends, kin, neighbours or daily routine. Part of the 'environment's' legitimacy in 'post-industrial' societies, and the consensus about its importance, stems from its importance as a 'safety valve' on the margins of urban life. In most LDCs promoting conservation objectives implies much more interference with poor rural people, whose environmental activities are designed to secure a livelihood rather than profit. Environmental management is a means of enforcing social control, not a means of escaping it.

Finally, and most importantly, environmental managerialism takes as given the distributive consequences which market processes and state power produce in the course of development. By divorcing 'environmental' from other distributive objectives, environmental managerialism helps to ensure that those who are well placed to avoid contact with the planning machinery do so, while those who are closest to the most severe ecological problems (desertification, deforestation, water contamination, and so on) are most likely to be uprooted and relocated. By locating the structural problems of underdevelopment in geographical space, usually in areas inhabited by the poor, environmental managerialism does not raise distributive issues in the development agenda, but serves to obscure them behind technocratic 'solutions'.

An example: environmental management in Mexico

Environmental problems have characteristics which make for relatively easy diagnosis but difficult solutions. Among the difficulties encountered is the complexity of different variables in the pattern of causation. Thus, agencies which wish to duck reponsibility for environmental policy can usually cite a confusion of evidence about causal factors.

In addition, most environmental intervention has to be undertaken within inappropriate time horizons. It is impossible to evaluate most environmental interventions within a time frame of a few months. It is also difficult to implement environmental policy in a brief period. These difficulties affect radical socialist governments as much, if not more, than conservative ones.

Finally, it is difficult to establish clear 'environmental' parameters and to measure, for example, the effects of changes in food systems on the 'natural' environment. It is not unknown for government delegations to arrive at international conferences on 'the environment', declaring that in their country 'environmental problems are secondary to problems of food production, water supply and infant health'! Fortunately, such curious platitudes are increasingly subjected to the criticisms of environmental activists within the Third World.[21]

The diagram on the following page represents some of these issues for one country, Mexico. In the first column the national

Environmental management in Mexico (1984)[22]

Plans and development programmes	Environmental components of plan
1. Global Development Plan	– reduce pollution
2. National Programme for Agriculture and Forestry	– conserve renewable natural resources
3. National Plan for Tourism	– maintain 'nature' for human access
4. National Plan for Urban Development	– to develop natural resources for human settlements
5. Energy Programme	– to protect the environment from energy growth (especially petro-chemicals)
6. Urban Development for Federal District (DF)	– to reduce urban pollution
7. Others e.g., Plans for Agro-Industry, Fisheries Industry, Education, Co-operatives, Housing, Science and Technology.	

Implementation

Different plans often have contradictory implications for the environment, e.g. the agricultural development plan (2) is geared to incremental growth, the energy (5) and tourist plans (3) imply reductions in growth.

Public administration of development plans is organized sectorally. Problems and solutions are inter-sectoral.

No specific provision is made for environmental programmes within public expenditure budgets.

The strategy and instruments for implementing the various environmental objectives remain undefined. No provision for environmental impact studies.

Limited fiscal measures against polluters and few efforts to reduce pollution.

'Biosphere Reserves' established by CONACYT in Durango, Jalisco, Quintana Roo and Sonora incorporate local populations in conservation activities. These show great potential.

Source – Information for Alejandro Toledo, *Como, Destruir el Paraiso*, Centro de Ecodesarrollo, Mexico City, 1985.

plans and programmes with some 'environmental' content are listed. In the second column the 'environmental' components of these plans are specified. The column below these refers to the implementation of these plans.

Several conclusions emerge from an exercise of this sort. Clearly different plans carry contradictory implications for the environment. In some cases economic growth is the objective, in others it is amenity or conservation. Furthermore, these contradictions are present within sectorally defined planning activities, as well as between them. The plan for agriculture, for example, seeks to promote a continuing increase in agricultural growth *and* the conservation of renewable natural resources.

Many environmental problems, of course, are inter-sectoral in nature, and shared between different ministries and government departments. Environmental programmes are also under-funded, undefined and scarcely ever properly evaluated. Where measures exist in law to prevent environmental damage (from pollution, for example) the agencies whose responsibility it is to ensure enforcement usually lack professionally qualified people and political muscle. There is neither the expertise nor the political backing for decisive action on environmental degradation. Much public sector policy implementation in poor countries is heavily dependent on political bribes, not merely as a means of buying electoral support, but often simply as a way of disbursing funds which would otherwise remain unspent (and eventually 'returned' to central government). The benefits to be derived from implementing environmental measures are often relatively intangible, while the financial advantages which public sector employees can gain from powerful economic interests opposed to environmental measures are very real indeed.

Defining an alternative project: from theory to practice

An alternative to environmental 'managerialism' needs to address several questions that are never raised within the conventional approach. First, it is necessary to demytholygize the view that environmental management is free from political bias. Political conflict is at the very centre both of the environmental 'problem' and of attempts to devise solutions to it. Second, an alternative project clearly needs to specify the *context* of local resource conflicts. As Blaikie (1984) argues,[23] environmental problems need to be contextualized: the alternative is an avid reductionism which ultimately holds the poor responsible for 'their' environment. Third, we need to specify the political resources available to different interests in the local environment, rejecting the idea that any 'optimum' solution can be implemented which is at variance with the interests of dominant classes, the state and the international economic context.

The 'environment' that is in the process of construction in LDCs today is separated from our own by underdevelopment. It is differently located, not simply in geographical terms, but in terms of its role in the development process. It follows that the 'environment' in LDCs is an arena for different social aspirations and material struggles. Most environmental struggles in LDC environments are concerned with the conflicts between the interests *in* the environment of emerging social classes. Our task is first to understand these conflicts and second to develop alternative action capable of strengthening the position of those groups which favour popularly managed, resource-sustainable solutions. Technical inputs will have a role in the search for solutions, but there is no 'technological fix' capable of regenerating the environment and resolving social and economic problems.

A start needs to be made with structural policies, in areas like prices, agricultural credit and fiscal incentives. At present these policies seldom advance the interests of the poor or their environments. The relationship between changes in structural policy and needed technological changes needs to be specified much more clearly. Where do they leave the environmental actors, the combatants on the rural stage?

In addition, an alternative project needs to take indigenous knowledge much more seriously than at present. If structural policies can be devised which allow the poor a larger stake in the management of their environment, then it is *they* who will have to do the managing. There are two reasons for this: they are the people who understand their own environments best and, ultimately, they are the only people in a position to implement sustainable development.

This raises other issues. Norgaard (1984)[24] has argued that indigenous knowledge 'uses an evolutionary epistemology in a world view that directly clashes with the epistemology of modern science and of modernization'. The challenge is therefore to scientists and technologists as well as to policymakers and political leaders. The rewards of learning from other cultures' experiences of conservation are considerable, as McNeely and Pitt (1985) demonstrate.[25] Efforts must be made to build this experience into environmental projects, rather as environmental impact assessment and cost/benefit analysis are built into projects today. It is also important to appreciate that indigenous knowledge is often lost in the course of severe ecological degradation. Anthropologists and others can play a role in ensuring that, like the 'raised-bed' systems of Tenochtitlan, what is lost to history is not lost to humankind.

Environmental change has both a contemporary and an historical dimension. These dimensions are usually overlooked in the desire to profit from developed country experience by adopting a 'managerialist' approach to environmental problems. This 'managerialist' approach is partly the product of our (historical) view of 'nature', and partly the product of regarding the environment as separated from the development process. When capital is dedicated to the transformation of 'nature', the social forces released are part of the process of environmental change. They need to be part of our analysis and part of the solution. They constitute the means of creating value and, potentially, of recreating democratic environmental politics. What is required today, especially from those who count themselves on the left, is an alternative project which locates the 'management' of the environment within a broader political economy approach. This alternative project must be adequate to conditions in New York and Berlin – where political ecology is largely a matter of the brain and the heart. But it must *also* be adequate to conditions in Mexico City and Jakarta, where political ecology is largely a matter of the stomach.

5. The Inner-city Environment: Making the Connections

Jeremy Seabrook

The distinction between the inner-city, the suburban and the rural environment appears at first sight so obvious as to require no comment. The scarred Victorian streets around the redeveloped heart of the city with their decayed mansions now multi-occupied, their demolished streets exposing an inside wall with ancient firegrate and shreds of wallpaper flapping in the wind, the buddleia and willow-herb that have taken root on the edges of the improvised car-park, the sooty shells of abandoned chapels, ruinous schools and Gothic pubs, the broken glass and rusting metal of derelict factory premises are familiar enough. As indeed are the concrete canyons, draughty walkways and vandalized garages of those geometric slabs of flats that were to have transformed the old inner-city landscape for ever, that vision of a better world of only a generation ago already corroded, spoilt and showing the clear lineaments of another, and even more intractable kind of poverty from that which it was to have effaced for ever. What stronger contrast could there be between these sad scenes, deserted of their very reason for existence, and the ordered symmetry and regularity of 1920s and 1930s suburban streets, with their flowering cherry and crazy paving and timbered gables and hydrangeas and illuminated chiming doorbells, and those more recent estates, with open-plan gardens, dwarf conifers and picture windows revealing such perfect interiors that they look more like shop window displays than homes? And the difference again between this suburban style – the dominant one in Britain now – and the overgrown villages that are spreading out to meet it, with their modernized stone cottages in the village centre which have long ceased providing shelter for the agricultural labourers for whom they were built and are now smart commuters' homes, with their exiguous council houses in which most of the longer-established village families now live? The difference is pronounced, if less dramatic, even though the glimpse of Georgian elegance, or of the Victorian villa with its holland blinds and wistaria, the rickety farm gates and the vista of ripening

corn under the cumulus sky of August, still provide illusions of
quite distinct and unchanged patterns of country life.

And yet the lives of most people have been shaped, in our time,
not so much by the physical setting in which they are played out,
but by another kind of environment, created by modern technology
and conveyed directly into the domestic interior. The images of
television, the homogenized products of mass marketing, the
shared products and universally accessible entertainments, the
information diffused by a limited number of centralized TV
stations and newspapers, create a far more unitary experience for
the whole population, independently of where they live. In this
sense, the power of the environment – in the more limited context of
the physical landscape – as a major determinant on the lives of
people is exaggerated; at least, it is far less significant than it was,
say, during the early industrial period. If we were not more
susceptible to the images, symbols, even the fantasies of a universal
marketplace than we are to what is actually going on in our
immediate vicinity, it would never have been possible for us to have
tolerated the physical transformation of the British landscape that
we have seen: the tombstone-like geometricality of the tower
blocks, the ugly swirl of the ring road, the glass and metal cubes, the
vast ex-urban sprawl, the uprooting of the hedgerows, the prairie-
like cornfields, the dying trees.

This perhaps is why, at least until recently, we have considered
the degradation of the environment (or rather, its continued
degradation – the criticism is as old as industrialization) a matter of
secondary importance. It has been felt to be a small price to pay for
the improvements in the living standards of the majority of the
people. Furthermore, there are many who now regard the place
where they live as merely a staging post: the mobility of people on
the new estates is tied to an inexorable progress up some career
ladder or other, and the home is merely an arbitrary and imperma-
nent halt on an upward trajectory. It scarcely matters what the town
is called, where we do our shopping or where we pay our rates: our
work will soon enough summon us elsewhere. There has been a
ruining of a sense of place. And those people who are the least
mobile – those tethered to the council house on the run-down estate
by unemployment or poverty – have, for the most part, the option of
turning their backs on the smashed glass, the boarded-up windows,
the vandalism and the rubbish swirling through bleak streets, and
finding consolation in another environment, that benignly furnished
by Lorimar, of Denver or Dallas or Beverly Hills.

What this means is that we must define far more sharply what we mean by 'environment'. It has been too easy for the political parties, having exhausted their thin and depleted rhetoric, to turn gratefully to the newly discovered issue of 'the environment'. We are all green now; but there is no doubt that this is for the most part mere image-making, a cosmetic adjustment on the edge of policies which will lead inevitably to accelerating impairment, erosion and spoilation of the planet.

Current references to the environment suggest something inert and passive, something external to us, 'out there' – surroundings, setting or decor. It is a wholly inadequate account of what is essentially a dynamic relationship between our fragile tenure of the earth and our use – or abuse – of it. No clearer examples could be found of this unimaginative and pedestrian definition than those attempts of recent decades to 'landscape' or upgrade some of the blemishes left by the period of early industrialism in Britain. This has principally involved the planting of saplings, which seldom seem to grow beyond the stage of being staked to birch-posts before they perish; the grassing over of slagheaps and pitheads; the demolition of acres of mills and factories; the turning over of warehouses to leisure centres, small enterprise units or restaurants, and replacing the gutted centre with multi-level shopping malls, with exotic vegetation, marble pillars and concealed lighting accompanied by an oppressive micro-climate, muted music and the shuffling of thousands of feet. There is no doubt that these attempts to beautify some of the most blighted and ugly habitats that human beings have ever been called upon to occupy has resulted in a transformation of sorts: the monuments to the industrial era have been substantially removed. Indeed, looking at these stunted versions of Arcadia imposed upon the old city centres it sometimes looks as though they were designed to efface the idea that the industrial revolution ever happened at all, as though it had all been a figment, a nightmare from which we have at last escaped.

The easy definition of environment sees the inner city and its poverty as simply a residual problem, a question of ameliorating the position of those left behind in the more general experience of post-war improvements. This view sees the resumption of economic growth as the source of hope for the inner city: as more wealth is created, the conditions in these places will get better; economic progress will automatically eliminate the minority who remain poor.

And yet the inner city remains the site of the greatest

concentration of all the major social and moral problems that plague contemporary western society. Here, there is a higher incidence of crime and violence, there is more psychiatric and emotional illness, there is more loneliness, there are more people on drugs, more people without work and bereft of marketable skills. It becomes increasingly clear that another, more sombre analysis of the inner city gains plausibility: namely, that far from being a vestigial problem, the poverty of the inner city is structural, a necessary, precise concomitant of the patterns of growth and development of the economy on which we depend to provide a remedy for those ills. Certainly, the most cursory look at the depth and intensity of inner-city misery gives the lie to any optimism that there is anything easier or more bearable about present-day poverty: the brutalities that attend it match anything that disfigured our social life in the first industrial period.

On the seventh floor of a long block of maisonettes built in the late 1960s with identical turquoise doors and reinforced glass balconies, and looking down onto a muddy grass square where dogs – owned, it seems, by no one – prowl around the discarded rubbish, lives Mrs Tyrrell, former mill worker and widow. Mrs Tyrrell no longer goes out on her own. She waits for her nephew to collect her on Fridays to go and fetch her pension. A neighbour from the next floor visits her once a week and does her shopping. Apart from that, she sees no one. Two years ago, she was robbed and attacked by three girls. One knocked at the door and told her she wasn't feeling very well; could she please have a glass of water? While Mrs Tyrrell went to the kitchen, the two other girls rushed into the living room and took her purse. When Mrs Tyrrell tried to stop them, she was knocked over and hit her head against the leg of the table.

She says, 'I'm frightened. This isn't a home, it's a prison. I'm sentenced to stay in, and what for? For the crime of being old. I'm not the only one. You can't pick up a paper without reading of somebody else who's been beaten up, tortured, knocked about, just because they're old and defenceless.' Her door is barricaded with two bolts, a safety lock, a chain and a spy-hole. She says bitterly, 'That is my security. I always thought when I was old my security would be my family, my flat and my bit of pension. But there it is.'

Under the flats, beneath the projecting balconies, most of the garages are unused, the doors twisted and buckled. The sheltered walkway at this level is unused, because it is unsafe. It leaves the apertures of the garages as a shelter for brief sexual encounters, for the homeless to sleep in, for the kids who run away from home, and above all, as a haven for early teenagers. Here is the perfect place for Jimmy's glue- and solvent-sniffing parties: torn plastic bags, empty tubes and tins, dented beer-cans. There are seven or eight young people, most of them about fourteen. They talk excitedly about the sensations to be had from getting high. They shrug off its damaging effects: 'He hasn't got a brain anyway, it can't make him any worse.' One tells of a boy who thought he could fly, another who rides up and down the lift-shaft in the flats on top of the lift. There is a slightly hysterical and hyperactive quality to their talk. They have been deeply affected during their childhood by the succession of marketed excitements that have been held out before them, permitting them neither stability nor rest in their growth and development. Avid for new sensations and experiences, it is the most natural thing in the world for them to turn to the forbidden pleasures. Indeed, they are the most faithful respondents to a culture which has nurtured them and which stands in a fair way to destroying them.

Kathleen is thirty-two. She was the victim of a sexual attack in the garages one night when she was taking the dog for a walk. She had bought the dog partly to guard the flat and partly as a pet for her two sons when their father deserted the family.

'But the children could never be bothered to take the dog out, so naturally I was the one who had to do it. Every night about six o'clock, I used to take it round the block. One night, half-past six, a man in a balaclava helmet and a combat jacket – I though he was a terrorist – he just grabbed me, put a hand over my mouth and dragged me into the garage, and him and his mate just raped me four or five times. He must've been waiting for me. They kicked the dog, it had to be put down. It must have been somebody who knew me. The thought they could still be prowling around upset me that much, I went to the doctor, and he gave me tablets for my nerves. I'm still on them, after three years. I can't do without them now. I never go out after dark. I'm frightened of all men, I'll cross over the road if I see a man coming. I found myself resenting the kids; my social worker said it was because they were both boys, I was taking it out on them, because they were male. I asked to have them taken into care for a little while. They can't forgive me. They don't understand.'

It is two weeks before Christmas. Betty and Chloe are both single parents, Betty with three children, Chloe with two. Chloe has lost her benefit book. 'It's going to be Christmas and I haven't got a penny to get anything for the kids. They want bikes. I know what I shall do, I shall go round the estate and nick two between now and Christmas Eve. Some Father Christmas. But that's the only way they're going to get anything. I don't see why my kids should miss out just because I haven't got any money.'

Upstairs, the flat is in chaos. The five kids have been playing together. Dingy, tumbled bedclothes litter the rooms; there is a strong smell of urine from the stained foam-rubber mattresses that are on the floor. Everything is used up and destroyed: dolls with broken arms; teddy with head torn off; sweet papers and empty crisp packets; crayonning on the wall; the light switch has been pulled out of its socket; all the plaster has crumbled away. Betty has been writing to a man in prison. He was someone a friend of Chloe asked her to write to. The letters became progressively warmer and more intimate. He asked her for a photo of herself in a short skirt; she wrote him her fantasies. She took the kids to visit. They liked him and said they wanted him to be their new Daddy. Betty was already making plans for the wedding. Then, shortly before he was due to come home, the social worker called. It appeared that he was in prison for molesting children. His wife had abandoned him. If he came to live with Betty, she was told, her children would almost certainly be subject to a care order.

In the local paper, there is a story that a woman's body has been found on the edge of the estate by two teenage boys. She was thirty-six years old, a wife and mother. The detectives are reported as saying they believe there are no suspicious cirumstances. Bill, unemployed engineering worker, says, 'Oh bloody aren't there? What's bloody suspicious is what drives people to do these things. Poverty and unemployment, they're the first suspects. There's plenty of suspicion as far as I can see, and I'm no sodding detective. It's society that killed her, only they'll not do anything about that. If they can't pin it on some individual, it's nobody's fault.'

Ramesh came to work in the mill from north India in the late 1960s. The mill closed in 1981, and since then he has been out of work. He lives with his parents, his brother and sister-in-law and their children. He is in his late thirties, sombre and full of regrets. They have bought their own house, but the payments are so high that they can no longer afford to go back to India to see the rest of the family. The house is a rather ramshackle Victorian villa in a street that overlooks the flats, rambling and draughty, although Ramesh has worked with friends to repair it and make it habitable. The family has been the object of attacks from youths on the estate: graffiti in indelible red paint over the top of the window, bricks through the glass. Ramesh has had to seal the letterbox because lighted, petrol-soaked rags were pushed through late one night. He says angrily, 'Do they think we closed their bloody mills? It was only us coming that kept them open a few years longer. What have they against us? I always say hello to my neighbours. Why don't they see that we are all in the same boat together, all workers unemployed?'

The boys in the local pub don't mind telling you they hate the blacks. Their conversation is full of 'jokes'. 'It only costs 35 pence to get rid of each one. We could get shot of them all at 35p a time.' 'How's that?' 'That's the price of a bullet.' 'They had special boats to bring them here. We'll have special boats to take them back, only we'll pull the plug out as we wave goodbye.' 'If they got rid of all the blacks in Britain, there'd be two hours extra daylight a day.' The rhetoric is the bragging machismo that masks despair: the de-skilling and disemploying of male energy, the rejection of their youth and vigour that has no immediate and tangible cause.

The estate was built in the 1960s, specifically designed as an improved environment, replacing the back-to-backs and the squalor of the Victorian city. It stands now as a kind of monumental denial of the visions of the early socialists and *their* environmental preoccupations, for had they not asserted that all that needed to be done was to change the surroundings in which people lived in the industrial areas and all social problems would miraculously disappear? That the human transformations have not occurred in sympathy with the rearranged setting, that those high expectations have been dashed, has given the greatest satisfaction to those who support the existing capitalist order, and who triumphantly declare that it proves there will always be people who cannot – or will not – avail themselves of the abundant opportunities they are offered to lead a decent life. They look at the social evils of these places and conclude that in a society which has become so wealthy, those who fail must be, not victims of the system, but disordered or faulty individuals. Because so many people have been able to get out, to buy their way into the suburbs and into private ownership, those who do not do so must be in some way defective. This is the sub-text inscribed, as it were, beneath the graffiti that disfigures the brutal landscapes of the inner city. In other words, capitalist society, with its abundance and display of all the heart could desire, and a great deal more besides, has been perfected; only certain individuals are unworthy of it – those who will not live up to its demands and imperatives.

In this way, the inner city does not represent a remnant, a residual problem, for the rich societies of the west. It is an essential component of capitalist society. The poor of the central city areas and the rundown peripheral estates are the product of a new international division of labour, the result of a global restructuring of capitalism. They are a minority in the rich countries, but their more numerous kin make up the majority in the slums of the cities of the Third World, and it is for this reason that the black population of Lambeth and Toxteth, the North African inhabitants of the HLM (Habitations Loyer Moderée) in Lyons and the satellite towns around Paris, and the people of the ghettos in North America have a symbolic role. The poor areas of the urban west are places of deterrence and fear, which exist to goad on the rest of the people to get richer, to energize them so that they will spare no effort to do anything that will preserve them from those infernal places of violence and misery. For without such a motivation, where would the will come from for the majority to strive and struggle for more? For all the talk of incentives in capitalist society, a far more powerful determinant upon our conduct, a far stronger fear and means of discipline, is the fear of what might happen should we sink into the abyss which seems constantly to be widening at our feet. The inner city is the material embodiment of an ideology which claims that we do not have enough resources to make the lives of all our people bearable. In a society where even the richest are always insisting upon their subjective feeling of insufficiency, where even the most well-off have perfected the art of pleading poverty, rich and poor are easily united in the illusory fiction that more, much more, of what we have now is the only answer to all the social evils that beset us. In other words, what we most urgently require for our deliverance is the intensification of those patterns of global economic development which have themselves produced that peculiar form of what Illich calls 'modernized poverty' in the richest societies the world has ever known.

It is in this sense that the word 'environment' has a vibrancy and resonance that goes far beyond the rhetoric of those who speak as if conservation were simply a question of fencing off sites of great natural beauty, or ensuring the survival of threatened animal and plant species. For the processes that are built into the perpetuation of the cruelties of the inner city are inextricably and dynamically linked to the exigencies of world-wide capitalist growth. The destiny of the rich is indissolubly linked to that of the poorest of the earth.

In the first industrial age, the machines that produced the wealth were propelled by the physical labour, the energy and muscle of the people in these industrial cities: we were yoked, tethered to the engines of production, and compelled to live at the remorseless and inhuman pace of the machinery we served. In more recent times, we have internalized those rhythms: rather than our reluctant labour being harnessed to drive the machine, we ourselves have become the demand for its ceaseless mobility, we have identified our needs with its necessity. Rather than being tied to it by our labour, we in the west now drive it by the fuel of our desires. This means that our far more willing compliance in maintaining its perpetual motion has been successfully sought. Such gains as we have made have been possible only because the production of much of the wealth has been removed from the old manufacturing areas of Britain, has been conjured out of sight to the slums and shanties and sweatshops of the Third World. Here the environment, so memorably delineated by de Tocqueville, Engels, Mayhew and Booth of Victorian England, has been recreated in identical detail in the *chawls* of Bombay, the *favelas* of Sao Paolo, the slums of Manila. This is where the environmental problems of the inner city have their roots, and why the poverty there remains so intractable. It persists because so much of the labour that debilitated body and spirit of the workers there in the nineteenth century has been exported to all the free trade zones, the offshore manufacturing sites, the agribusiness empires in South East Asia and South America, and because so many of the things we take for granted as objects of daily use in the west depend upon the subordination of people, not only in the rich world, where settled ways of life are constantly being uprooted and patterns of labour altered, but even more so in the factories of Taipei and Seoul, the mines of South Africa, the plantations of the Philippines, the ranches of Central America, where peasants are evicted from subsistence farms and traditional patterns of living disturbed in the interests of providing the global rich with what they have come to regard as their 'needs'. There is a symbiotic link which unites the de-energized, functionless and deskilled youth of Handsworth, Moss Side and Liverpool 8 with the ceaseless activity of the youth of Calcutta, Mexico City and Jakarta, whose energies are used up gathering rags, waste paper, plastic and metal, scavenging to survive, fetching and carrying for others, working in sweatshops twelve hours a day, never earning enough money to buy the food that will replace the effort expended in the day's labour, and sleeping the sleep of exhaustion at the roadside, wrapped in dun-coloured rags among the fumes and noise of the traffic. In both cases, the energies of the young are wasted – in the one case by having nothing demanded of them, no purpose or function, and in the other by doomed and destructive efforts to make a sufficient living. Both are casualties of those intensifying world-wide concentrations of power and wealth whereby 200 corporations control one-third of the global product.

The peculiar horrors of inner-city life – and we should always remember that for all the victims and the suffering, there are also many millions of people who lead lives of quiet heroism and fortitude, who rise above the mulitude of injuries that are daily visited upon them – cannot be understood in isolation from those developments which not only determine their misery but are also at the root of endless disturbance and violence and injustice elsewhere in the world. It is often said that the people of the inner city have, for the most part, been excluded from what the rest of society accepts as 'normal' – the habits, tastes, desires and customs of the majority. But those habits and customs are structured in such a way that for their continued satisfaction, the latter must continuously go on dispossessing the poorest of the earth in accelerated and aggravated forms. This is why they cannot be regarded as 'normal', but as part of processes that distort and exploit and ruin the lives of those who share with us all too briefly a fleeting and always menaced sojourn on the beautiful and fragile integument of the planet.

This is why the political project in relation to the environment is a far more profound and epic undertaking than any mere conservation or landscaping of the inner city can convey. For it involves the search for a more stable relationship between the people of the earth and the people with the earth. And that, in turn, means the seach for sufficiency: an ancient dream of security and a modest plenty, that would ensure that no one wants for shelter, food, warmth, education and leisure. It is a most frugal goal, accessible to all humankind, but one that has been buried, a petrified dream, under the tumultuous lava from the volcanoes of industrial productivist activity, both capitalist and existing socialist. The simple aim of *enough* has been effectively bypassed by capitalist civilization, for the idea of enough is the most radical threat to a system that depends absolutely on *more*, independently of its quality or future consequences. But if the poor are to be rescued from chronic malnutrition, sickness and insufficiency, then this modest ideal will have to be resuscitated, as a crusade, not only for the poor but also for the rich. For both it would represent a liberation. It would rid our rich societies of the diseases of their excesses, the over-indulgence of a wealth that brutalizes, and redeem that waste of human resources which are locked up by money just as effectively as the poor are debilitated and denied and depleted by the lack of it.

It can be seen that there is the possibility of a joint global project which does not set the rich world in endless competition with the poor, but which is based upon a shared liberation of the two. In this way, the young, underemployed and begging on the streets of the Third World city, whose counterparts suffer from the rejection of their wasting powers and possibilities in the inner city of the rich world, can be united in a common cause. It is in this sense that the meaning of saving the environment springs into urgent life, for it is a question of the survival of all of us.

Part Two:

Building Social Environmentalism

'I am convinced that discussion between socialists and ecologists, if conducted frankly and in public, will not lead to division but will bring together all those elements that have an eye to history, and above all to the future.' (Rudolf Bahro, 'Unite or Destroy the Earth', in *New Statesman*, 18 January 1980)

6. Radical Environmentalism and the Labour Movement

David Pepper

'The left are no better than the right, and the centre is the worst of the lot.'[1]

I want to argue here that this view of British party politics and their relevance to radical environmentalism is simply not tenable. Clearly there is a move among environmentalists in groups like Friends of the Earth to recognize the highly political nature of what they say, and of what they seek. But as yet their political critique is insufficiently developed and their political effectiveness, undeniable as this is, not as great as it might be. This effectiveness could and should be enhanced by recognizing that most radical environmentalist aims are probably inherently socialist by nature, and certainly are not compatible with *laissez-faire* capitalism as propounded by the present Conservatives in Britain. Thus, without working for a form of socialism we are unlikely to attain an ecologically conscious and harmonious society. However, it is a form of socialism – anarchist rather than centralist – which is not in the mainstream of the present labour movement, and for this reason, as well as others which I shall detail, this movement has many deficiencies from an environmentalist point of view. Nonetheless, environmentalists must, as well as continuing pressure-group politics, take a more overtly party political stance than they do at present – at least as individuals if not as groups. And despite Labour's shortcomings this stance should, I believe, take the form of working for the labour movement (the Labour Party and the trade unions) and working to promote change within it.

Inadequacy of the present political stance

Several things worry me about the present political stance of many environmentalists. To begin with, it seems to have little coherence or consistency, except that based on the lowest common denominator of dismissing all except the British Green Party on the grounds that the others, unlike the greens, have nothing new to offer and that newness is all.

Thus, despite the assertion that 'greens are notorious for their courtesy and open-mindedness', spokesmen like John Morrissey can be pretty discourteous and bigoted when it comes to politics:

> Greens should clearly understand that Labour is encumbered by a century's worth of obsolescent philosophy; that it has inherited inescapably narrow perspectives deriving directly from a political analysis evolved in the nineteenth century; that it cannot divest itself of its history and traditions . . . and that it can become no more Green that a tortoise can become a hare. The increasingly elastic boundaries of socialism will not stretch far enough to include Green politics. 'Green' or 'libertarian' socialism is political nonsense, and 'Green Socialists' are either bogus, or they have been caught with their trousers down in the wrong party.[2]

This kind of rhetoric seems fashionable among those of a green persuasion. In 1983 the Ecology Party told us: 'The politics of class consciousness are at an end', and 'The Politics of Life [whatever they are] start here'.[3] In 1984, Jonathan Porritt informed us that 'The old system is bankrupt and it is only the wisdom of ecology which will show us how to create a new economic order . . . green politics have something totally different to say . . . there is an integrity about green politics that fits ill with the machinations of contemporary politics.'[4]

The rejection of the 'old politics' is part of another worrying trait – that is, the elevation of the idea of 'newness' to an almost sacred principle and a quasi-religious belief in the inevitability of transition to a new culture – as expressed, for example, by Frank Capra:

> The social movements of the 1960s and 1970s represent the rising culture which is now ready for the passage to the solar age . . . our current social changes are manifestations of a much broader and inevitable cultural transformation [during which we must] . . . go beyond attacking particular social groups or institutions, and show that their attitudes and behaviour reflect a value system that underlies our whole culture.[5]

The lack of class perspective here is remarkable from one who wants to mount a massive threat to the owners of the means of production, distribution and exchange. But more than that, as Pender rightly points out, Capra's 'talk of paradigms lost and regained seems little more than an ecological recycling of sixties notions'.[6] Of course, where Capra comes from, in affluent, professional Northern Californian 'Ecotopia', the 1960s never really went out of fashion. Pender goes on to sum up the objections to this instant-fast-philosophy-new-now approach (also scathingly denounced by Murray Bookchin):[7] 'The green's cult of modernity, of newness, is deeply disturbing. It seems to reflect the very consumerism which they seek to reject: ecology is the brand new product in the political market place.'

If Capra rehashes the 1960s, Porritt rehashes the 1950s. In slagging off 'industrialism' rather than capitalist forms of indus-trialism, and in lumping the left and right together as the proponents of 'industrialism', to which only the greens are opposed, he revives 1950s convergence theory. As described in Chapter 1 of this book, this theory held out the prospect of 'the end of ideology'. As greens have presented it since the late 1960s, the 'new' ecological 'crisis' was so grave as to 'transcend ideology': pollution, overpopulation and resource shortages would get us all, regardless of whether we were left or right, middle or working class. Instead of class struggle, the only struggle we were presented with was 'green' versus 'industrialism'. This was the message of the late 1960s environmentalist,[8] and for some it is with us still. In attacking 'industrialism' and in making no distinction between its capitalist and (potential) socialist forms, it focuses attention on the *technology* of pollution, resource depletion, and so on, and not on who owns and shapes it, nor the social relations that stem from it. This is all part of a wider problem environmentalists have, which Pender calls a 'surprising lack of interest in the history and origins of their ideas', and it is starkly illustrated in Porritt's contention that: 'This dual emphasis on decentralization and internationalism is quite unique to the green perspective.'[9]

By this staggering assertion, Porritt may mislead us into forgetting a whole lineage of socialist and populist thinkers who, as we saw in Chapter 1, emphasized both decentralization and internationalism – Kropotkin, Proudhon and Godwin, the anarchists, and utopian socialists like William Morris and Robert Owen, not to mention the Diggers and Levellers. As Pender put it, in response to the co-chairman of the Ecology Party Paul Elkins's indulgence in 'the favourite eco-sport of rubbishing all the established parties':

To lump the Tories together with the Labour Party as if they are equally culpable and equally useless is to ignore the latter's positive achievements – most notably the creation of the welfare state [surely the most wide-reaching environmental measures ever enacted in Britain]. No one can lightly dismiss the struggles and hopes of the generations who have fought in the labour movement for an ideal of economic and social justice, for international co-operation, equality and freedom, including freedom from the threat of war and from the horrors of industrial exploitation: an ideal which, in short, bears a very strong resemblance to that of the greens themselves.[10]

This lack of historical insight is really a lack of political insight. It comes out in a number of unfortunate ways; for example, in some greens' approach to economics and employment. If you do not have the physical or mental benefits which come from work, or if you do work but in an alienating way so that the division of labour and the production line make you just 'an appendage to a machine', then your living environment is impoverished – there can be no doubt – and Schumacher, the greens' guru, has stressed this.[11] Most socialists who I know stress it too, and maintain that since production – the social act of transforming nature – is a defining characteristic of being human then all humans *should* have meaningful work as of right. However, one sort of green response to the unemployment problem is typified by a letter in *New Ground*,[12] proclaiming that the real 'unemployment problem' is

. . . joyful. It is that modern technology has reduced the need for wage labour. Splendid news. More time for leisure activities – so long as we can keep eating. The 'right to work' and the creation of jobs is nonsense. Most jobs are drudgery, therefore the problem is to share out what work there is whilst ensuring that everybody keeps eating . . . The Labour Party needs to acknowledge that none of the 'isms' are effective and to think out new policies suited to the age of the computer and robotics . . . It needs better brains than mine to work out the details.[12]

So say all of us to the last comment – it matches the banality of the rest. That regards as 'splendid' the inevitable tendency for capitalism to substitute capital for labour, always producing an 'industrial reserve army', and deduces that because most jobs are drudgery we would do best by not working, having more 'leisure' and sharing the profits of machine-done labour. There is no disposition to consider *why* jobs are drudgery, for example through deskilling – another inherent feature of capitalism – nor that unemployment and job alienation are all part of a process whereby one section of the community maintains its privileged position in a power hierarchy that will no more redistribute fairly the fruits of machine (or human) labour than it will give up its capital assets (like land and other resources) to communal ownership. In short, there is no political analysis in this green perspective, so there is no believable political programme. Indeed, the forum for green 'alternative' political economic analysis, TOES (the other economic summit), frequently fails even to discuss capitalism, seeing it as irrelevant to the 'new' economics. There is, according to Anderson,[13] no clear understanding of how economics – the economics of the prevailing system, which is capitalism – mediates and organizes the human-nature relationship. This is borne out by Paul Elkins, director of TOES, who, in presenting the deficiencies of 'conventional' (not 'capitalist') economics,[14] never once mentions capitalism. He rejects an 'economics' which sees the earth as an infinite source of resources and a waste sink, which assumes financial gain as our main motivator, which recognizes only effective demand and not human need, which proposes growth as a universal panacea and is not concerned with work quality – but he does not recognize these characteristics as inherent in capitalism. Conversely, he proposes a 'new' economics of steady state, of liberation from unemployment, of personal and collective self-reliance, of human need rather than effective demand, and of concern with ownership of the means of production and what the mode of production does to people and the environment (the relations of production). He does not recognize in his 'new' economics the elements of anarchist socialism.

But I would maintain, once again, that we have here nothing 'new' at all but rather a form of economics which is not only compatible with anarchist socialism, but which could not arise without it, for it is socialist economics.

Socialism and environment

Why this is so, I have argued elsewhere;[15] and I have also analysed the social and economic changes which environmentalists like Schumacher, the Ehrlichs, Schnaiberg, the *Blueprint for Survival* and the Ecology Party have proposed.

Their proposals have displayed, to an extent at least: (i) an awareness that what constitutes 'natural' resources and human 'needs' is not absolute, but is definable only in relation to specific historical modes of production and cultures; (ii) that there must be wide-scale resource redistribution (achieved partly, in the Ecology Party's view, by ending private ownership of land); (iii) that the prevailing mode of production (capitalism) cannot continue but will inevitably demise; (iv) that future production must be non-alienating (of people from people, or from the things they make, or from nature); and (v) that a decentralized small-scale economy is the best form of social organization for achieving ecological and personal harmony. Although these proposals and perspectives have not been based on any very explicit or strong class analysis, they nonetheless have, I think, embodied much of an essentially socialist view – when, that is, socialism is defined as 'a social system based on common ownership of the means of production and distribution' which displays an 'attachment to ethical and democratic values' as well as 'an emphasis on the distinction between common and state ownership'.[15]

In practice, this kind of socialism, which is substantially part of a western intellectual tradition rather than a definition of what is found east of the Iron Curtain, belongs to what Ward[16] also defines as an 'anarchist' rather than 'centralist' tradition. As I shall acknowledge, this tradition has often been subordinated to centralism in the British labour movement, but to claim – as Morrissey does – that because of this 'history shows that the central dynamic of socialism is collectivist, statist and anti-libertarian, and bears no resemblence to the green alternative' amounts to a too-easy dismissal of the Kropotkin-Godwin-Owen tradition to which I referred above. This branch of socialist tradition advocated a decentralized, small-scale, self-sustaining Britain, where human needs are satisfied by minimal use of energy. Industry and agriculture are combined in its communities, and handwork and brainwork are combined in each individual's work – the production line and division of labour having been largely abolished. Production is not for profit, but for social usefulness – products are not commodities for exchange but they embody the kind of social relationship between producer and consumer which is part of a deeply felt community relationship. Individuals are important, but true individual freedom can be realized only through relating to others, in the manner of Rousseau's social contract, for example. Also, while the small community acts locally it 'thinks globally', as the green slogan has it, and indeed communities may federate for specific purposes, including interaction with other nations. But there is no centralized national government, no nationalism, and much reduced international trade. Power is largely devolved to democratic communities in which everyone collectively takes policy decisions. A labour-intensive society in which all do socially needed work produces an intensively used and peopled landscape, where the urban-rural distinction is blurred, and industry, as small factories and workshops, is scattered throughout the countryside. Such was Kropotkin's anarchist vision,[17] which, in detail, corresponds closely with that of the seminal *Blueprint for Survival*,[18] published seventy-three years later in 1972, and with Callenbach's *Ecotopia*.[19]

This is not to say that the evironmentalist utopia is founded on the same principles as that of the anarchist. It is important to recognize that whereas the latter proceeds from the notion of radical social and economic change to benefit all *people first*, the former was proposed primarily in order to kowtow to 'ecological laws', and bolstered not socialism but an environmentalism that was, as we saw in Chapter 1, largely an elitist defence of what a minority of ex-urbanites saw as 'wild nature' or 'traditional landscapes'.[20]

More recent versions of ecotopia, however, have seemed less elitist, and have even more in common with the anarchist socialist tradition. Indeed there is an occasional direct link with this tradition. Ebenezer Howard, who initiated and inspired the Garden City movement, was himself, it is said, influenced by Kropotkin and by William Morris (whose *News from Nowhere* was a romantic socialist vision of a future along anarchist and 'ecological' lines). In 1978 Lord Campbell challenged the Town and Country Planning Association to create a new garden city. In response, the Association proposed a city incorporating Howard's (anarchistic) concepts of

> settlements of a small human scale; a basically co-operative economy; a marriage of town and country; control by the community of its own development and of the land values it creates and the importance of a social environment in which the individual can develop his own ideas and manage his own affairs in co-operation with his neighbours. The Association thus proposes a garden city in which an optimum level of independence and self sufficiency to the community from its surroundings and from larger-scale bureaucracy would be fostered – notably in the fields of community finance and land ownership, employment, energy and food supplies, education, health and construction.[21]

In turn, all of this has been translated into the proposals for

'Greentown' in Milton Keynes – proposals which are replete with the ecological as well as the social imperative and which represent a seamless welding of nineteenth-century anarchist socialist ideals with twentieth-century ecological ideas. So too does the model for an ecologically sound village community of the future which was based on studies by the Dartington Institute.[22]

There are other similar links which can be made between socialist principles, and practice, and the kind of economy and society which modern ecological writers like Schumacher and Capra advocate. For example, the Mondragon co-operatives in Basque Spain are often quoted by environmentalists as examples of ecologically sound principles in action.[23] They were directly based upon the ideas of Robert Owen, founder of paternalistic socialist communities in nineteenth-century Britain and America. In them, capitalist values of private ownership and profit, and treating nature and people's labour merely as commodities, were subordinated or eliminated.

None of this is to say that either environmentalism or socialism is, or should be, primarily concerned with evangelizing an ideal blueprint for the future. (Indeed if socialism, guided by Marxist principles, concerns the liberation of people and therefore their ability to guide their own destiny for themselves, then by definition it cannot rigidly prescribe how people shall live.) Rather, much of the attention of both environmentalist and socialist writers is correctly devoted to a critique of existing society. What I think the environmentalist critique at present lacks, however, is a sufficiently developed political dimension. On the one hand it starts off with similar principles to the socialist critique – a dissatisfaction with capitalism and a belief in its inevitable demise (see the *Blueprint*), plus a feeling that in order to escape from environmentalism's justifiable[24] middle-class image 'it is crucial for environmentalism to see, and to articulate to others, the links between environmental issues and human beings, and the links between environmentalism and economic and social injustice'.[25] But on the other hand it does not follow through the political implications of its own findings.

For example, environmental abuse is seen as an outgrowth of much-despised values, which are often vaguely attributed to 'industrial society' and/or even to Christianity.[26] These values include the notion that progress, individual and social, is measured solely in terms of material improvement and attained through consumerism. They include the social Darwinistic ideas that competition and struggle, rather than co-operation and mutual aid, and 'natural' and therefore justifiable ways to behave. They include the idea that 'objective' scientific rationality is a superior approach to knowing nature and other people than are the 'subjective' approaches, which allow intuition, emotions and feelings to play a large part in determining our actions. And they include the odd idea that the right privately to own resources like land, water and visual amenity, and thereby to exclude others from these resources, is sacred and God-given. Many greens will rightly attack such ideas, but they do not then follow through by asking *why* they hold a deeply entrenched position in our society, while other opposing ideas which they prefer are marginalized and not seen as 'common sense'.

Socialism, however, does ask such questions. And it answers that the prevailing ideas in society cannot be considered in isolation from the 'economics of the epoch' (incidentally, this does not mean that the former are determined solely or even largely by the latter). The fact that a certain set of ideas and values prevails over another set must be related (albeit in a complex way) to the fact that it reinforces in some way the material vested interests of the 'ruling' class of people. In capitalism it is the owners of the means of production (land, buildings, machinery, stocks and shares, and so on) who stand to gain most from the conventional wisdom that competition and individualism are 'good', as are private property, the work ethic, the accumulation of consumer goods or the exploitation of nature.

The corollary of this is that even if we – as informed, enlightened, well-off, middle-class greens – might ostensibly be able to 'mend our ideas' and radiate inner beneficence towards our fellow creatures (furred, feathered and human), the majority of people will certainly do nothing of the kind so long as they are part of a capitalist mode of production that supports a capitalist conventional wisdom which has seeped deeply into our culture. This has been borne out by what some see as an eclipse of mass environmental concern in the west since the early 1970s. As economic recession has overtaken the majority of people, so that majority has reaffirmed its central values of materialism and consumerism. What has been happening to 'nature' – the nature of countryside and wilderness rather than human nature – has been of marginal concern in the scramble to maintain or regain material positions.

Of course, it is the *practices* which flow from these much-despised values, described above, that really harm 'nature'. Some of these practices relate to industry's desire for short-term profit maximization, even though part of the source of that profit (for example, the soil, or the stock of minerals) may be destroyed in the long term. They relate to capitalist society's clear distinction between 'private' and 'public', enabling private industry to try to internalize the profits of its operations and externalize its losses to society and environment as a matter of good business practice. (Thus the entrepreneur can keep most of the profits of agribusiness farming or road haulage, while the government (taxpayer) picks up the tab for clearing the effects of nitrate fertilizer out of waterways or concreting over thirty acres per mile of farmland to build motorways – and all, of course, including the young, collect the costs in landscape deterioration or lead and particulate air pollution.) And, most fundamental of all, adverse environmental practices will stem from industry's push for the kind of material economic growth supported by the vast majority of people – a growth based on the throughput of raw materials rather than their recycling or conservation. But I think a socialist would say that none of these practices stems simply from 'industrialization' or production of itself – at least the greens have nowhere convincingly shown that this is so. We can say, however, that there are inherent features of the capitalist organization of production which are going to produce such practices: they certainly *do* result from capitalist industry. This being the case, whatever other conditions are necessary, we can be sure that the elimination of capitalism is a prerequisite for the elimination of the environmental evils which flow from this kind of economic organization.

This, of course, is a very old-fashioned political sentiment. But I think that many greens will agree implicitly with it, even if they do not wish to be so immersed in the 'old politics' as actually to admit it. However, the question then is: how will such radical change be achieved, and who will achieve it? In the elitist and idealist view, it can be done by a group of intellectuals and well-meaning, socially motivated people who, by dint largely of thinking about it, will be the vanguard of a revolutionary change in mass consciousness. They will bring us to some 'post-industrial' (non-industrial?) future of unimaginable leisure and greater wealth equality where, in place of the high material standards that many regard as a right today, *all* will experience relative poverty but without 'misery', revelling instead in the nebulous concept of 'quality of life' (itself highly reflective of white Anglo-Saxon Protestant values). This is a rather self-indulgent and reactionary view, for the mass of people do not figure in the kind of ecological utopia it projects. It is not merely difficult; it is nigh-on impossible to imagine Cowley car workers, Sunderland soccer fans, Brixton bomb throwers or even Cheam commuters fitting into the sickly, self-congratulatory, sanctimonious, tree-hugging communities of Callenbach's *Ecotopia* or *Ecotopia Emerging*. And who would blame them for not doing so?

All of it is, in fact, too idealistic[27] – that is, it assumes that social change will come about largely through people changing their ideas and values. As the *FoE Supporters Newspaper* editorial (autumn 1985) put it: 'FoE is seeking to bring about change at a deeper level – change in people's attitudes and values.' As such, these sentiments are largely hogwash, for they presume that there can be a 'miraculous creation of the ecologically-conscious human being via some cathartic, unspecified revolutionary experience'.[28]

Profound social change will not happen like this. On the one hand, it may be encouraged by the kind of campaigns which organizations like FoE, Greenpeace and CND are so expert at. There is a good case for continuing pressure-group campaigning. It undeniably does influence people's ideas, and it is important to seek this influence. But on the other hand, such campaigns do proceed from the assumption that we live in a pluralist democratic society in which the government – any government – almost automatically responds to mass campaigns by conceding to some of their demands. Thus, in this view, government policy evolves partly in response to ideology, but also partly as the child of electoral pragmatism. Such an evolution brought us in the past the notion of 'Butskellism' – that compromise between left and right which brought about many of our current environmental ills and which has been translated into modern SDP-Liberal Alliance politics (which also claim, falsely, to be 'new'). But today little such evolutionary pragmatism is evident. Instead we have the no-U-turn non-compromising politics of Thatcherism. Pressure groups do achieve success, but these are largely the groups which represent the ideology of the ruling class: for example, the M40 Support Group, or the road lobby in general, or the Channel link consortia, which have managed to influence the government to the extent that the 'democratic' institution of a public inquiry has not even been held over the Channel tunnel project. If other pressure groups, like the anti-nuclear or anti-motorway organizations, present any serious threat to the ruling ideology and class, then they can forget pluralist democracy. They will not make, and have not made, any very substantial headway against the aspirations of the Thatcher-Reagan axis and the enormous financial interests which it represents.

The exception to this, as I shall suggest below, might have been in the area of local politics, where Labour had won power. But as we know, much of this success was temporary, lasting only as long as it took for the Conservatives to take away local democracy by rate-capping and indeed by abolishing those councils which opposed them.

In these circumstances, environmentalists must choose a course of action which will lead in the short term to the removal of the Thatcher-Reagan axis, and in the longer term to nothing less than the removal of the capitalist economic system which nourishes it and which it nourishes. This must, at least partly, mean political action of an 'old-fashioned' party political sort. And, in the light of what I have said above, it must mean action to secure the return of a Labour government, the advance of the labour movement, and the promotion within it of truly socialist (socialist anarchist) principles and policies. For, as I have also argued, Robin Cook's assertion that 'There are strong areas of congruence between socialist and ecological theorists in their rejection of the capitalist organization of production'[29] is true. So also is Neil Kinnock's view, that

> Democratic socialism – the collective control and organization of resources under the collective control and organization of democracy – should be the most natural political conviction for all who care about the environment.[30]

Clearly this is also a conviction towards which Charles Secrett of FoE moves when he talks of the need to bring agriculture and forestry under greater public control, giving the wider community a democratic right to comment on, suggest alternatives to, or deny if necessary, developments which 'demonstrably affect their environment'.[31] Neither Kinnock or Secrett advocates anything which has to lead to the centralist, almost totalitarian form of socialism of which so many environmentalists are afraid. But it is a long way from this convergence of ideas and beliefs to actual green support for the currently constituted and disposed labour movement in Britain. However, I cannot see that greens have much choice about crossing this particular bridge between theory and practice. On purely pragmatic grounds it is important to continue pressure-group activity, but on these grounds it is important also to have in power the political party which is most likely to be receptive to the pressures which are set up by greens, and to respond accordingly. Because of the congruence of theory discussed above, that party must, fundamentally, be Labour. At the same time there must be an awful lot of work within the labour movement to strengthen the kind of socialism which greens want to see. Such work will be more effective than criticism from without in achieving change. Environmentalists cannot rely simply on the electoral appeal of their policies to 'green' the parties in a meaningful way, for in a time of economic depression anti- rather than pro-environmentalist policies are more likely to have mass appeal.

But in order to be realistic we must not underestimate the magnitude of the task. Clearly the labour movement has major shortcomings in its approach, from an environmentalist point of view. Green socialists within and outside the movement – in organizations like the Labour Countryside Group or the Socialist Environment and Resources Association – are only too aware of this, and the following section reflects their concerns particularly.

The labour movement's environmental shortcomings

Given the analysis of socialist theory that the root causes of environmental exploitation and abuse lie in capitalism itself, the most serious charge against the labour movement is that it does not sufficiently attack these root causes and concentrates instead on the easy targets, like pollution, which are merely symptoms. To the extent that this is true, such a failure might be a reflection of, first, the Labour Party's 'clientist' approach to the environmental and other lobbies; second, the party's adherence to economic growth; and, third, the trade unions' desire to share in the profits of capitalism and to stick at that.

Clientism, according to Carver,[32] has characterized the Labour Party's approach to the electorate since the last war. It involves the attempt to attract different interest groups into voting Labour by concocting a manifesto 'shopping list' of measures which will appeal to lots of diverse groups (witness Neil Kinnock's skilfully disguised shopping list in his 1985 Conference address: appealing to peace groups, feminists, business entrepreneurs, pro-Sandinistas and so on). This is really treating the electorate as 'consumers' of policies, while manifesto preparation is largely a matter of updating such policies to keep them attractive – for example, to the radical professional middle classes who make up much of the environmental lobby. In no way does a manifesto so derived constitute a coherent plan which will make Labour an agent of sustained social and environmental change such as will attract true greens – one which alters the country's economic and social structure by, for example, initiating widespread worker co-operatives.

Hence, Labour's 1985 *Charter for the Environment* attacks pollution, but not capitalism – state and private – for seeking to maximize output and profit while externalizing environmental costs to society at large. Indeed, output maximization, albeit for 'social need', is a major plank of Labour Party policy, whose 'Alternative Economic Strategy' (AES) argues for exponential economic growth (3 per cent per annum on the GNP). Not that Labour is necessarily at fault for demanding growth. Many environmentalists, including greens, have moved on from the days when economic growth of any kind was seen as mortal sin, and this is an important advance for those who want to widen the 'green' appeal. Of course much poverty could be eliminated via the socialist expedient of wealth redistribution alone, within and between nations. But it is unlikely, to say the least, that no further economic growth of any kind is needed, and that it is all a matter of wealth redistribution. And, conceivably, certain forms of economic growth are acceptable, desirable and environmentally benign. Clearly many services, including education and health care (especially preventative), need to be expanded under a green programme, and there should also be manufacturing growth in Britain, based on co-operative and holistic principles.

However, the doubts about Labour's economic growth programme stem from the fact that it is not this kind of 'alternative' green-socialist growth which appears to be advanced. Rather, it seems to be the same old indiscriminate growth which places emphasis on GNP as the standard of living indicator rather than on other indicators which include environmental costs and benefits.

Cook puts this case well in an attack on the AES.[33] Labour's record on ecological issues is 'wretched', he concedes, recalling the support for Concorde – 'a giant leap backward in socially useful technology'. And if, with the AES, *all* that the Labour Party wants is faster growth then it deserves Schumacher's taunt: 'British socialism has lost its bearings and presents itself merely as a device to raise the standards of living of the less affluent classes faster than can be done by private enterprise.' Cook reminds us that socialism should have richer aims, which spring from ethical revulsion at the exploitation of people by their fellows – and the exploitation of people is inseparable from environmental exploitation. Hence an Alternative Ecological Strategy, as well as an economic one, is needed. Labour, says Cook, should be considering quality as well as quantity of growth.

That this frequently does not happen is exemplified by many trade unions. In their concern to protect jobs, they ignore the possibility that some technologies are potentially too dangerous and costly to be continued. Thus Gavin Laird, AUEW Secretary, enthusiastically joins Social Democrat MP Robert MacLennan in backing the proposed nuclear reprocessing plant at Dounreay. As a *New Ground* editorial put it: 'There is a danger that some trades unionists may, in the long term, be siding with capital, helping to sow the seeds of a poisoned future.'[34] A grotesque example of this occurred in the legal action brought jointly by Hoechst Chemicals management and the trade union IG Chemie against West German Green Party members who spoke against Hoechst in Frankfurt City Council.[35] Another occurred at a Labour Conference fringe meeting in 1984, when NUM Secretary Peter Heathfield, sounding like a Conservative government spokesman, asserted that the environmental damage done by acid rain had not been conclusively established, and that environmental pollution could not anyway be abolished because of the costs involved. Here, indeed, are regional class alliances[36] being made between bourgeoisie and proletariat in defence of national economic interests which run against the interests of the wider international community. This kind of alliance leads greens to deduce that trade unions have a vested interest in existing economic arrangements rather than in replacing them by some other arrangements, like socialism. Unions' power and influence is seen to derive from how successfully they defend jobs and economic status against capital in a worker-management/boss relationship. Hence, the unions are regarded as a drag on any radical tendencies in the Labour Party, because although the party is a coalition of interests – peace activists, feminists, blacks, unions, MPs, constituencies – overwhelmingly disproportionate voting power is given to the unions and far too little is given elsewhere.

However, even if unions did want jobs at any price, they are likely to be disappointed by the AES which, Robin Cook asserts, promotes capital rather than labour-intensive growth, based on high technology. As Wagstaffe and Emerson say,[37] Labour's 1983 manifesto, with the TUC's Economic Review, proposed *labour-saving* growth, accepting that full employment would no longer be possible. 'Such are the ideological triumphs of the defenders of capitalism that even its enemies have been seduced into believing

that a job for everyone has become an unattainable goal in practice
. . . the entire [Labour] movement has accepted the false
assumptions of an outdated set of economic ideas.' It is scrambling
to get back to full employment capitalism, without considering
fundamental socialist (and green) questions about the very nature
and purpose of work. Work must be for satisfying social need rather
than for commodities for profit – and if it is truly to be 'production
for people' rather than vice versa, then alienating, deskilled labour
on the production line must be eliminated.

In fact, only socialist planning and perspectives are likely to lead
us towards this radical shift in the nature of work. It was, after all,
the socialists of the Lucas Aerospace Shop Steward Combine and
the Transport and General Workers Union (TGWU) who, in 1976
and 1983, produced the most radical and far-reaching proposals
that have been seen in decades for replacing work in polluting and
dangerous technologies (for example, in nuclear power and nuclear
weapons) by alternative production (see Chapter 3). But, despite
Labour's 1985 *Charters* for jobs and environment, the question
remains as to whether the party is serious enough – or socialist
enough – on this issue. As suggested above, a decentralized socialist
country may best be able to achieve 'production for people', yet it is
doubtful that the AES seriously envisages this. There is, says Cook,
talk of a host of new local co-operative initiatives, but the AES also
betrays a parallel commitment to centralized planning, 'expressed
as a riot of acronyms – an NIB, an IRF, an NPC and a more
powerful NEB'.

Colin Ward[38] believes that the tragedy of the British labour
movement lies in its 100 years of strong centralism and neglect of
the anarchist tradition discussed above. The centralists – the
'zealots of the left' – have given Reagan and Thatcher their
triumphs, and are still doing so, for example in Liverpool Council,
whose leaders have actually fought against and stopped the city's
pioneering housing co-operatives, in Weller Street and Hesketh
Street.

Similar centralist tendencies have beset the consumer co-
operative movement. Despite a rearguard action by the National
Federation of Progressive Co-operatives, in recent years there have
been strong moves to create twenty-five large regions out of 100
separate co-operative societies, and to merge the Co-op Retail and
Wholesale Societies into one. And while socialists have discussed
decentralization, Labour governments – like Attlee's for instance –
have set up some giants of centralization, like the National Coal

Board (NCB) and the Central Electricity Generating Board. They have thus played into the hands of a Tory press which depicts socialism as totalitarian and remote from people.

Thus 'the state' as a remote Orwellian monolith has come to be synonymous with Labour in popular images, although socialists (and greens) are fundamentally the enemies of the state. The distinction between monolithic state ownership and common ownership ought to be visible in, of all things, Labour's policies for the land – but it is not. What Labour has done has been to establish state landlords, like the Ministry of Defence, the NCB and British Rail, which have managed land badly and have not given people control over it. What Labour has not done has been to make any significant progress towards common ownership and control of land. Although the Labour Land Campaign produced a draft Bill for common ownership in 1984, it is unlikely to appear in the next manifesto – whereas something similar did appear in the Ecology Party manifesto in 1983.

Thus there is scope for criticism of Labour's environmental stance on fundamental grounds – that it is no more committed to the removal of capitalism than are the other parties. There is also a widespread view that the Labour Party's professions of concern for environment are empty rhetoric: mere cosmetic attempts to garner the green vote. Despite Neil Kinnock's insistence that environmental policies must be integrated with social/economic policies, 'the environment' is still seen as an issue which Labour relegates to the periphery. Despite the plethora of 'environmental' motions which now go for compositing at Party Conference, the environment is not yet conceived of as an integral part of Labour policy. For some, the appointment of John Cunningham as shadow environment spokesman hardly engendered confidence in the seriousness of the party's approach, since he, as MP for Windscale, was a major opponent of an anti-nuclear stance. Said to be in the pocket of BNFL, he expressed no doubts, in 1984, that nuclear generation of energy was here to stay. Neither did he apparently protest greatly when Labour's National Executive Committee's study group on the environment was axed.[39] Mistrust of this kind was again engendered by an individual when, in 1985, Gwynneth Dunwoody agreed to act as Parliamentary consultant to the British Fur Trading Association. Predictably, this led greens to ask 'How can the Labour Party claim concern for the environment?'[40]

But even with the best of intentions, could Labour carry out its environmental policies? Carver thinks not,[41] because it will not have truly mass support for these policies – merely an electoral majority – and because any popular mobilization around socialist ideas has usually come from outside the party and not from within it – for example, from the Independent Labour Party, the Clay Cross Councillors, and other radical groups. Such groups have been either peripheral or an embarrassment to the mainstream. O'Brian,[42] who advocates a Labour-Green alliance, imagined a familiar scenario. A Labour government, elected in 1987 or 1988, would be faced by an export crisis because North Sea oil production would be falling and because Britain's manufacturing base would be shattered. It would try to reflate, by housing and other infrastructure projects, and by regenerating domestic demand, but despite or because of this there would be a big import increase and the basic economic crisis would not be solved. In such a scenario, environmental policies would have zero priority – indeed, nuclear power could become a cornerstone of the attempts to revive industry on a 'cheap' power base. Certainly there would be few prospects of resisting the powerful political lobbies which are environmentally damaging, like the road or agribusiness lobbies.

Then why support Labour?

The answer to this question, as has been argued above, is partly pragmatic and partly a matter of principle. That their support for the labour movement would amount to more than just making the best of a bad job for greens can be suggested in three broad ways. First, notwithstanding the accuracy of some of the criticisms described above, considerable progress has already been made in 'greening' the labour movement's attitudes and policies. Second, though we cannot expect a full-blooded socialist programme from a Labour government – probably not in the twentieth century – we will get further along the road to socialism through Labour than we will through alternative political parties and strategies. Third, the labour movement has that breadth of vision which can set green policies in the context of broader social and political policies, therefore, in the long run, making them appeal beyond a middle-class clique.

The greening of Labour
The Labour Party's 1983 manifesto made some important promises in areas of deep concern to greens. It made commitments to workers' co-operatives and job conversion; to massive energy

conservation, spending on renewables, combined heat and power schemes, and stopping the pressurized water reactor programme; to a host of measures for countryside conservation and rural services' improvement; to inner-city investment for health and homes; to pollution control, recycling and public transport investment. Although the 'shopping list' ethos was clearly present, and a coherent environmental strategy was lacking, that shopping list was impressive. It reflected growing environmental concern in Labour – and indeed the penetration of Labour by green activists. The pressure has since grown, with calls from many constituency parties in the 1984 and 1985 Conferences for a significant part of the manifesto to be devoted to ecological issues. These have been backed by at least twenty motions per year on the issues which were in the 1983 manifesto. Canterbury CLP, for example, called for a ban on nuclear dumping and plutonium exports, and a freeze on nuclear power with a programme to develop alternative jobs for power station workers; the Buckingham CLP called for a programme to bring agricultural land into public ownership as part of a general plan for protecting the rural environment and creating rural employment.

Such pressure has not been in vain, for the movement's expressed commitment to environmental policies has grown. In 1985, for example, the TGWU delegate conference voted to seek closure of all nuclear power stations and the planned and safe cessation of all other nuclear establishments, except those for disposing of already created wastes. There was, too, a pledge for ensuring new jobs for those affected. This is important because without such pledges a cause like this would probably encounter stiff opposition. The TGWU was the biggest in a long line of unions which came out against nuclear power in the early 1980s – the NUM, NUPE, NUJ, COSHE, UCATT, SPOE, NGA and ASLEF were among the others. Later on in 1985, Jim Slater of the National Union of Seamen persuaded the TUC Conference to support a philosophy of seeking forms of economic growth which do not harm the 'natural' environment as well as curbing those forms of growth which do harm it. The Conference backed coal production but opposed the PWR (Pressurized Water Reactor) programme. It stopped short of opposing all nuclear power, but it is unlikely to be long before such total opposition becomes a reality. Certainly, also in 1985, the Labour Party Conference called, by four million to 2.5 million votes, for a halt to the existing nuclear power programme and for phasing out all existing plants. This was not the two-thirds majority which would have put this policy automatically into the manifesto, but political commentators believed that it would be increasingly unlikely that Labour would oppose the PWR programme without also opposing AGRs (Advanced Gas-Cooled Reactors).[43] Labour also committed itself in 1985 to an Environmental Protection Agency, a Minister for Conservation, tight legislation on toxic emissions and acid rain, and an inquiry into the health and environmental problems around Sellafield, in addition to existing environmental policies.

But it is in the field of action rather than talk that some of the most convincing arguments lie for green support for Labour. Encouraged by environmentalist campaigns, elements in the movement have struck practical blows for environmental policies which have been far more valuable than many more publicized 'non-political' demonstrations, car-sticker campaigns and petitions.

It was the seamen's union, backed by ASLEF, the NUR and TGWU, which forged an alliance in 1983 to stop the British government dumping nuclear waste at sea. The same union told its members, after the *Mont Luis* sinking in 1984, to refuse to allow any radioactive material on passenger ferries or other non-specialist transport ships. And trade unions have come together with environmental groups to oppose the privatization of water authorities and hospital ancillary services. The first measure would, they believe, further lower rates of investment in sewer construction and maintenance, leading to sewer collapse and flooding – and to gastro-enteritis outbreaks following the pattern of those which happened in Belfast, Hull, Bradford and Bootle in 1982–4. Hospital privatization, according to NALGO, NUPE, ASTMS, and GMBATU, would lower standards of food and other hygiene, giving hospitals a less healthy environment than at present.

Much of this kind of action was not initiated by the unions, or born out of unprompted environmental concern. They had, for example in the sea dumping case, to be subjected to intense lobbying from Greenpeace and FoE before acting. But, as I have suggested above, they *did* respond to pressure, seeing at least in part that their own vested interests were at stake and the convergence of these interests with environmental concerns. However, one might legitimately add that they also responded to green pressure groups because they did not on this occasion identify as closely with the interests of free market capitalism as some of the green critics imply that the unions do. This kind of responsiveness can be further developed, provided that environmentalists do not confront the unions but seek to explore common ground – not least of all in the appeal to fundamental socialism, for many union members still do believe in socialism!

The Lucas Aerospace plan for alternative production, developed in the mid-1970s by shop-floor workers and academics, continues to reverberate around the world. In Britain it led to the Centre for Alternative Industrial and Technological Systems (CAITS) at the end of the 1970s: in the mid-1980s Lucas and CAITS spawned, according to Elliot,[44] the Greater London Council's (GLC) alternative technology network, and similar projects in Sheffield and Coventry. In India, the Lucas ideas have been forged into an alternative plan for safe and socially useful production at the Bhopal factory, which was shut down by Union Carbide after the 1984 poison gas disaster. The remaining 632 workers were sacked, but they joined with survivors of the disaster to formulate the plan which is

> the first of its kind in India. It is also highly significant in bringing together workers, unions and ecology groups in a single campaign . . . the environmental organizations have been persuaded to take the workers' interests and the need for jobs into account: the unions are embracing concepts of community participation and accountability some distance from their traditional demands.

Now Lucas workers, CAITS, SERA (Socialist, Environment and Resources Association) and the Great London Enterprise Board are working together to help the success of this campaign.[45]

That action rather than mere words can come from the recognition of green principles in socialism, and vice versa, was further exemplified by the GLC. When this body was Labour-controlled in the early 1980s it took a score or more measures to improve the environment of millions of Londoners. Low public transport fares and the diversion of resources from roads to public transport were well publicized, as was the GLC's appearance at the Sizewell Inquiry to oppose the PWR programme. Other measures were more quietly enacted, like replacing asbestos underground train-brake shoes with non-hazardous materials; developing cycleway systems; transferring domestic waste from road to rail transport; strengthening the Council's Pollution Control Division and establishing an Ecology Unit; setting up thirty-six materials recycling centres; extracting methane gas from an Essex landfill site and using it to run a nearby board mill, and producing, through the

Greater London Enterprise Board, socially relevant employment through supporting workers' co-operatives and establishing the London Energy and Employment Network.

Again, it should be conceded that the Labour GLC did not always take these steps until years of pressure and leading by example had been applied by environmentalists. But eventually the leads *were* followed, the pressures *were* responded to; and far more by a Labour-controlled GLC than by the previous Conservative council. This principle, as I have said, is as valid nationally as it is at the local level.

The right road

If some of the above might be criticized for its lack of ideological purity or comprehensiveness, it might also be regarded as hopeful and positive. It sets us on the right road to improvements in environment and environmental consciousness, even if it does not represent the end of that road. If green concerns are inseparable from socialism, as I have argued, then the cynic is bound to observe that socialism and the labour movement in Britain are often not congruent. However, for socialists or greens to reject Labour on those grounds would be suicidal – for it would be to give up any possibility of their gaining a measure of true political power through a movement which is, after all, basically responsive to its membership. Without such power, diluted though it may be, there is less prospect of effecting even limited policy changes. Without *some* limited changes – without making a start, that is – there is little prospect for a gradual softening of public opinion from present indifference towards a heightened environmental consciousness. And an initial softening is needed before further and more significant environmental changes, which will themselves be catalysts to more radical shifts in opinion, can be made. Although it is not the only prerequisite, public attunement towards green ideas must accompany the change towards a green (socialist) society.

The experiences of nearly a decade of rampant, extremist Thatcherism should have taught us that some power with some principles is preferable to ideological purity in a political wilderness. We have, to an extent at least, to agree with Gavin Kitching,[46] in rejecting reliance on a strategy which (vainly) awaits cataclysmic events to promote sudden and revolutionary change towards pure socialism and 'green-ness'. Although I am arguing strongly for recognition in principle of the fundamental coincidence between socialist and green concerns, and that the latter cannot be met properly without the former, I must also support Kitching's more pragmatic view that 'if we have to wait for international socialism *before* nuclear disarmament or effective measures to check pollution of the seas can be contemplated, then the prospects for the human race look gloomy indeed' (emphasis added). Thus we may well have to opt for an alternative that will bring some power with some socialism, while still maintaining the integrity of our vision of what is ultimately desirable. Certainly, neither support for Conservative, Alliance or Green Parties, nor disdainful contempt for all politics, will achieve that.

Furthermore, those green activists who are suspicious of the Labour Party because of the record of its 1960s and 1970s administrations ought to consider more deeply what it was that the 'splits' and arguments of the early 1980s were all about. As Roberts points out,[47] most of them concerned precisely the issues that worried environmentalists, such as centralized versus direct democracy, workers' control and co-operatives, anti-capitalism, and disarmament and peace. Limited but probably permanent changes have certainly occurred, such as the strong commitment to a non-nuclear defence policy. Though compromises have had to be struck, the 'centre of gravity' of the party has shifted enough to the left to suggest that in government it will be truer to socialism than were the 'pragmatic socialists' of the past two decades. All this is good reason to join the party and redouble the struggle to maintain its momentum of change. For 'Labour won't change if those who are the most critical of its current practices abandon it to the statists and paternalists'.

This particularly applies to those who dislike the power structure in the movement which, I concede, must be modified. Again, recognition that too much power was vested in the parliamentary party, and in the unions, was a central issue in the arguments of the early 1980s. To an extent this power distribution is being altered, in favour of more direct democracy. The momentum of this change can be maintained by criticism from the outside, though more essentially from within. But a word of caution here: in their desire to further democracy, and in their sometimes justified suspicion of unions who have an ambiguous environmental stance (like the TGWU, who supported the NUS anti-sea dumping campaign but helped to breach the miners' strike) greens should not alienate themselves from the union movement. If we are to address the true environmental concerns of the mass of people, we must see them as they are: related ultimately to the wider concerns of the people, which are still voiced by unions.

Broadening out

This brings us to a central concern of this book, which is that it is high time that greens reviewed their own ideologies, which have been based on a rather elitist romantic bioethic. 'Ecological principles' have often been put first, as the fundamental basis for a reformed society. So people who are not interested in modifying their personal behaviour and thought patterns to accord with the view that they are merely a sort of animal have been excluded. Amidst all the talk of a 'new awakening', and gains in membership, there has been blindness to the fact that relatively few people are really 'waking up' to the environmental problems of the kind that groups like FoE, Greenpeace, CPRE or the National Trust are concerned with. Conversely, these groups have not woken up to the fact that most people *do* have environmental problems, of a different sort, caused by poverty, ill health, no work or alienating work, and alienating social environments. However, the labour movement came into being to solve exactly those environmental problems and if we should forget this we might re-read *The Ragged Trousered Philanthropists*. Rather than jumping on any green bandwagon, Labour is, in a sense, waiting for greens to wake up and jump on *its* long-rolling bandwagon. Only then will the mass of the people be interested in going green.

The 1985 *Charter for the Environment* is thus holding a consistent line when it stresses the need to create new jobs, to use planning controls to prevent pollution and environmental damage, to increase the democratic control over environmental decision-making, to be as much concerned about the urban as the rural environment, and to be concerned about the latter as a place of access for urban people. For Labour's environmental policies should remain, as anyone's should, firmly integrated into industrial and social policies so that they will be relevant to a much wider spectrum of people that those in the green movement. As Neil Kinnock stressed:

For us environmental campaigning concerns the urban as much as the rural scene. While we are committed to the protection of open space and the countryside and the promotion of the necessary measures, we want people to understand that the environment is an issue for everyone, not just those who live in the country.[48]

Green ideals, then, cannot be divorced from socialist ideals, and the latter cannot be divorced from the labour movement (though there is not total coincidence). Greens, therefore, should not be divorced from the labour movement. They would be foolish to continue the pretence that they are about a 'new' politics: rather they lend a new perspective to issues that are as old as the hills. In amongst the utopianism and romanticism, there are real political battles which need to be won, for the sake of the environments of the mass of the people. For greens disdainfully to refuse to join those battles, which the labour movement is fighting *now*, in defence of some supposed but un-thought-out higher ecological principle, would be merely a dereliction of fundamental green principles.

7. Mixing It: Energy, the Environment and the Unions

Kim Howells

The business of energy has always been located firmly in the cockpit of politics. Without consistent and adequate supplies of energy, no state can plan its future with any confidence.

Consequently, when the Organization of Petroleum Exporting Countries (OPEC) sprang its fourfold oil price increase on a largely unprepared world in 1973–4, planners everywhere began groping for alternative means of establishing secure and cost-effective supply systems. Frequently, they failed. Sometimes they attempted to construct mutually beneficial alliances. All too often they spun in panic like weathervanes in a storm and ended up jammed somewhere between the coal and nuclear sectors.

The trade union movement spun with them in equal disarray. The result in the UK is a kind of pentagonal TUC wrestling-ring, whose five corners are occupied by the champions of those working in the coal, oil, gas, nuclear and electricity industries. So powerful and violently suspicious are these combatants that the referee (normally the TUC general secretary) finds it healthier to shout his interpretation of the rules from outside the ropes.

Meanwhile, the energy bosses tear lumps out of each other in the various bear-pits between Millbank and Throgmorton Street. Occasionally, a forlorn cry tails off with the word 'environment', lost in the clamour of money deals and horse-trading. 'Jobs versus Environment' has always provided entertainment as a supporting bout. Rarely, if ever, has it attained star status for more than a relatively fleeting moment, as the controversy over Three Mile Island proved.

Nuclear politics

Outside the USA the majority of energy corporations and governments are peddling a line which claims that the malfunction of the Three Mile Island PWR was little more than a timely pause in the inexorable forward march of nuclear generation. In effect, they are *using* the 1979 Three Mile incident to support their own case for an expansion of the nuclear sector. They are saying, 'OK, we recognize that we underrated certain deficiencies and problems, but we've learned our lesson and now we're ready to confront the great challenge that awaits us and the rest of humanity: the provision of endless cheap energy from nuclear fission. We are ready to make that great dream come true.'

Inside the USA, the nuclear industry has been in deep trouble since the near-collapse of the domestic nuclear power station market in 1974. Massive cost over-runs and nagging worries about safety and shoddy workmanship have done little to convince the general public that it should believe the great promises made for this system over the years.

The pro-nuclear camp has split into two: the 'hard-liners' ('Forget Three Mile Island: nobody got killed') and the 'reformists' ('Three Mile Island was a design error compounded by human monitoring problems: we'll learn from it'). It is difficult to say which group is in the ascendancy. Mark Hertsgaard has analysed the split and concludes that the reformist position is becoming the more influential despite the fact that most senior policy positions in the Reagan administration are still held by hard-liners.[1]

Whatever the reality of that political power struggle, it is clear that most western European governments and energy agencies have realized that their plans for nuclear expansion are doomed unless they promote an image of themselves as belonging firmly in the reformist camp; particularly since the Chernobyl disaster.

Their position is made no easier by the failure of successive optimistic predictions about energy demand to materialize. Hertsgaard points out, for example, that electric utilities in the USA now have 30 per cent more generating capacity than the national grid requires (20 per cent is considered a safe margin) and he predicts that this ratio may well increase.[2] The situation in Europe is little different. Electricité de France (EdF), for example, has saddled itself with a large burden of overcapacity and an astronomical capital debt accumulated during the construction phase of its ambitious nuclear programme. Consequently, EdF is currently hawking cut-price supply deals around EEC energy markets in an attempt to claw back sufficient revenue just to service its capital debt. Our own CEGB, for example, has recently contracted to import EdE nuclear-generated electricity via two 1,000 MW cross-channel underwater cables, despite having admitted (virtually in the same breath that it announced the nuclear deal) that it is 'moth balling' several of its giant oil-fired stations because they are surplus to the CEGB's requirements.

In the meantime, of course, the shadow of the proposed Sizewell B PWR looms large. If it becomes a reality, the government has announced its intention to build PWRs at Druridge Bay, Hinkley Point, Dungeness and a second one at Sizewell. The electricity supply industry (ESI) has been enthusiastic since the heady days of 1967 about the prospect of a massive shift to nuclear generation.

The run-down of the coal industry intensified in that year and continued until OPEC flexed its muscles in 1973–4. By 1980, the ESI's dependence on coal had risen from 63 per cent in 1974 to 82 per cent. As energy expert Colin Sweet has pointed out, the

> attempted switch to nuclear proved a costly failure. But nothing appears to have been learnt, except that this was a policy priority that required massive manipulation of the facts and of public opinion . . . The ESI's role has been central to the formulation and execution of this strategy. Despite its best efforts to reduce its dependence on coal it is more dependent on it than it was ten years ago. Oil firing is too expensive to operate (but not apparently to construct).
>
> Nuclear power's contribution remains less than 20% and given that it is not acceptable to a large proportion of public opinion its future must be in doubt. It is therefore a tribute to the power of the energy institutions and to the inability of the decision making process to grasp the realities of change that the only investment programmes that the ESI have put forward have been solely nuclear. In 1978/79 they said 'After Drax "B" the programme will be exclusively nuclear.' And so it has been. Reactor choice has been a story of unparalleled confusion and waste. After switching to the PWRs in 1972/73, the CEGB switched back to the AGR, then back to the PWR. Now they are apparently prepared to ride the AGR in again, but this time on the back of the PWR if that is the only way to keep a nuclear industry alive.[3]

Save it for jobs

This waste and confusion has occurred against a shifting background in which government agencies are slowly beginning to acknowledge that the days of cheap energy supply may permanently be over. They are making encouraging noises about energy cost control and conservation. 'Energy management' is now recognized as an integral function of any sizeable commerical administrative or industrial organization attempting to optimize profits and efficiency.

The Secretary of State for Energy, Peter Walker, spoke in June 1984 of his department's aim to save £7 billion a year. This represents an average saving of 20 per cent of total energy consumption in the UK. To attain this objective, the minister has created an Energy Efficiency Office and claimed 1986 as Energy Efficiency Year.

Although these targets are reflected generally throughout the EEC Ten, they will not easily be hit. If energy consumption is compared with other economic aggregates, the rise in the Community's gross inland energy consumption rose in 1984, for example, by about 30 million tonnes oil equivalent, or 3.4 per cent from the 1983 level. This is a considerably greater increase than that in the gross domestic product (+2.9 per cent), private consumption (+1.1 per cent) and industrial production (+2.9 per cent). This increase effectively reversed a steadily less energy-intensive trend in the Community's economy over the period between 1979 and 1983.

Whether this reverse will continue is subject to speculation. Certainly, if governments meet their targets of improved energy management it is unlikely that any major upward shift in electricity demand will take place. Nor is there any likelihood that we will witness in the late 1980s or early 1990s a large increase in manufacturing and industrial production (and consequent increase in energy demand) such as we witnessed in the early 1960s. It is difficult in 1986 to locate any likely sources of easily available cheap energy which could play the role of catalyst for a similar period of economic expansion such as that played in the 1960s by oil imported from the Gulf states. The role is as unlikely to be filled by French nuclear generation or expanded Colombian coal exports as it is by a sudden deployment of solar power generators, wave energy converters or sophisticated windmills, however beneficial or otherwise we may consider these sources to be.

It is quite clear that the most fundamental shifts in energy requirements will arise not from revolutionary breakthroughs in the technology of energy provision or fuel pricing, but as a result of large-scale measures taken to improve the pattern of energy consumption by various savings and by using waste heat or renewable energy sources.

The Fraunhofer-Institute for Systems Analysis and Innovation Research in Karlsrühe undertook a study for the EEC Commission and concluded that a Community-wide energy-savings policy could mean a cut in demand of 120 million tonnes of oil equivalent (Mtoe) in addition to the expected saving of 300 Mtoe which would result from the EEC's 'Energy 2000' policy. It has been estimated that the implementation of these policies would lead to an increase of about 530,000 jobs by the turn of the century (based on increased future labour productivity).

The Fraunhofer (ISI) study concentrated its examination on four countries: Denmark, France, West Germany and the UK. Between them, they account for more than 70 per cent of the EEC's primary energy consumption. The researchers looked at the potential economic effects which might accrue from the application of the following six technologies:

1. district heating (in most cases using combined heat and power generation);
2. insulation of residential buildings;
3. heat exchangers for heat recovery;
4. large gas engine-driven heat pumps;
5. domestic solar hot water systems;
6. biogas plants in agriculture.

The analysis was based on the investment period 1983–2000 and on an assumption that these technologies account for only about one-third of the total additional energy saving potential in the Community. It predicted that insulation would account for more than 50 per cent of the potential savings, heat recovery about 20 per cent and district heating about 12 per cent. Biogas solar thermal systems and gas engine driven heat pumps would each contribute less than 10 per cent.

ISI did not study in any depth the various other energy conservation technologies like electronic control techniques, the improvement and the substitution of energy-intensive processes, organizational measures, co-generation in industry and the use of renewables such as wind, water, straw and wood. It is clear, however, that application of the six technologies examined could yield additional net employment of between 98,000 and 190,000 jobs by the year 2000. The specific net employment effects varied between 2,800 and 8,000 jobs per Mtoe primary energy saved, the average being 2,800 jobs.

Whether these and other savings will be implemented depends entirely on the degree of political pressure brought to bear on the EEC's decision-making bodies and, more importantly, on the governments and energy corporations of the member states. There will be a great deal of resistance from many quarters, notably from energy corporations like Electricité de France which need desperately to sell the product of their immense over-capacity.

Andrew Holmes and Michael Parrot have predicted that France will add 20,700 MW of nuclear-generated capacity to its existing 33,670 nuclear megawattage by 1988, with yet more nuclear stations to follow. By 1992, France will have a *minimum* nuclear generating capacity of 62,703 MW. In 1983, its *total* generating capacity was around 76,000 MW, including 20,000 MW of hydro capacity (planned to expand by 6,100 MW by 1990) and a considerable coal-fired generating capacity which was *enlarged* in 1984 by 1,160 MW.[4] It is reckoned that the French domestic and industrial demand for electricity will have to double in fifteen years in order to soak up the output of these new stations. All signs at present indicate that this will not happen. Moreover, the French experience is not unique. A number of other EEC and non-EEC European states have ambitious nuclear programmes either underway or planned. The EEC Ten's Summarized Energy Balance, on the following page, provides a detailed breakdown of projected energy demand and supply by sector.

It can be seen, quite clearly, that the two most spectacular categories of projected growth in indigenously produced energy are nuclear (76 Mtoe/215 Mtoe) and 'renewables' (1.67 Mtoe/7 Mtoe). Hard coal, oil and natural gas are all set to decline, though in terms of total inland consumption only oil is considered likely to suffer an overall decline.

Rigged choices

When set alongside the nuclear projections, the likely actual (as opposed to percentage) increase in renewable energy sources is derisory. If the summarized energy balance is even close to accurate, nuclear generation will have completely outstripped all other categories of indigenous energy production by the year 2000. In the first quarter of 1985, nuclear had nudged hard coal out of third position in the EEC primary energy production stakes, though the odds were distorted by the UK miners' strike. It is clear that the broad spectrum of anti-nuclear opinion should reassess with some urgency its perception of current and future developments in the energy field. A combination of at least two weaknesses has seriously impaired the ability of the anti-nuke forces to achieve significant advances in its campaigns to halt the expansion of nuclear generation.

Summarized energy balance – EUR 10 Energy 2000

(Mtoe)

		1973	1980	1983	1990	2000
I.	Gross energy consumption	968.04	970.05	907.21	1,034	1,136
	– Bunkers	37.36	26.21	21.98	28	29
	– Inland consumption	930.68	943.84	885.23	1,006	1,107
II.	Inland energy consumpion	930.68	943.84	885.23	1,006	1,107
	– Solid fuels	221.97	222.68	211.99	242	264
	– Oil	563.93	493.82	416.29	413	410
	– Gas	115.83	169.26	165.35	190	196
	– Primary electricity, etc.	28.95	58.08	91.60	161	236
III.	Indigenous production[1]	351.29	462.10	516.29	563	625
	– Hard coal	171.16	153.31	143.06	139	137
	– Lignite & peat	26.49	31.81	30.99	36	35
	– Oil	13.17	90.52	132.51	111	108
	– Natural gas	112.20	129.16	119.94	115	108
	– Nuclear energy	17.73	42.67	76.06	145	215
	– Hydro & geothermal[2]	9.38	12.39	12.00	13	14
	– Others & renewables	1.16	1.66	1.67	4	7
IV.	Net imports[3]	619.91	527.15	377.90	471	511
	– Solid fuels	19.00	47.28	39.08	67	92
	– Oil	596.21	437.95	288.78	330	330
	– Natural gas	4.01	40.56	48.17	75	88
	– Electricity[2]	0.69	1.36	1.87	– 1	—
V.	Stock changes[4]	+ 3.15	– 19.21	– 13.08	—	—
	– Solid fuels	– 5.32	– 9.72	+ 1.14	—	—
	– Oil	+ 8.09	– 9.03	– 16.99	—	—
	– Gas	+ 0.38	– 0.46	+ 2.77	—	—
VI.	Electricity generation input	235.13	279.06	286.73	367	444
	– Solid fuels[5]	108.33	130.12	138.38	160	178
	– Oil	75.04	60.91	36.86	20	18
	– Natural gas	23.51	31.31	21.76	27	15
	– Nuclear energy	17.71	42.67	76.06	145	215
	– Hydro & geothermal[2]	9.38	12.39	12.00	13	14
	– Others & renewables	1.16	1.66	1.67	2	4

Main indicators (related to the 1990 objectives)

	1973/63	1979/75	1990/83	2000/1990
Inland energy annual growth rates	+ 4.6%	+ 3.4%	+ 1.8%	+ 1.0%
GDP annual growth rates	+ 4.7%	+ 3.6%	+ 2.4%	+ 2.8%
Energy GDP ratio	0.98	0.94	0.75	0.37

	1973	1980	1983	1990	2000
Share of oil in gross energy consumption	62.1%	52.3%	48%	41%	37%
Share of coal and nuclear in electricity production	53.6%	61.9%	74.3%	83%	88%
Supply dependence on imports	64 %	54.3%	41.8%	46%	46%

* *Source* Statistical Office of the European Communities
* *Source* 'Energy 2000' study, DG XVII. November 1984.
1. Production of primary sources, including recovered products.
2. The conversion of electricity, including hydro and geothermal, is based on its actual energy content: 3,600 Kjoules KWh or 860 Kcal KWh.
3. The (—) sign means net exports.
4. The (—) sign means a stock decrease.
5. Including coke oven gas and blast furnace gas (derived from coal)

The first is a tendency to assume that the Chernobyl incident has torpedoed permanently the fortunes of the pro-nukes. As I've explained earlier, nothing could be further from the truth. Too much money, too much political investment and too many potential jobs are riding the nuclear horse for those who've backed it to change their faith. It takes more than a mere disaster to scare off the likes of Reagan, Mitterand, Thatcher and the Westinghouse, Bechtel and GEC engineering corporations. Chernobyl is old news. When it suits them, bankers and politicians have short memories.

The second weakness is an apparent willingness among many anti-nukes to mumble vaguely of 'renewable energy' 'replacing' our present energy systems as if the process could somehow take place between pints of real ale and sessions on the word-processor. Energy is big business. Very big, political business. It is frequently corrupt, stinking, dangerous and expensive. And we take it for granted. We flick a switch, turn a tap, press a button and we expect (and usually get) instant results. Anti-nukes will find it far from easy to convince a population with this level of expectations that there's anything seriously wrong with a system which invariably meets demand, even during the most difficult periods. (We in the NUM can bear painful witness to that fact.)

To convince public opinion that its anti-nuclear instincts are the right ones, those who oppose an expansion of nuclear generation must bridge a credibility chasm. We have to encapsulate our environmental arguments and analyses in a viable package of nuts-and-bolts proposals about the future provision of energy, warts and all. That means the greens mixing it with the miners, the power workers, the union bosses and the political mandarins. It means formulating clear policies which people can understand and in which questions of finance, jobs, health and safety, democracy and efficiency occupy central roles, rather than peripheral ones. The promise of the creation of 530,000 new energy-linked jobs rising from the application of energy-saving schemes might well prove a most effective hook for public opinion to bite on. It could certainly provide a focus for positive debate into which could be drawn all of the fragmented elements currently masquerading as a cohesive anti-nuclear alliance.

Similarly, it is hardly possible to imagine a more sharply focused subject for debate than the recent controversy surrounding the report of the all-party Commons Environmental Select Committee which indicted Britain's nuclear industry for its ineptitude in disposing safely of the country's nuclear waste. It had all of the ingredients needed for a comprehensive examination of the relationship between, on the one hand, the raw economics of energy production, the cost and dangers of reprocessing and waste disposal and, on the other hand, the enormous financial and employment resources inevitably committed to such undertakings.

The MPs' deep reservations on the key issue of reprocessing spent nuclear fuel reflected the great seriousness of the dangers involved in the whole process. But it was also quite clear that they recognized the political risks involved in ordering the closure of a project as costly as the Thermal Oxide Reprocessing Plant (THORP) under construction at Sellafield in the jobs-hungry Cumbrian region.

Their worries and reactions are mirrored faithfully inside the trade union movement. It simply isn't the case that elected union officials are ignorant of the environmental issues at stake. Rather, like the rest of us, they find it no easy task to present viable employment alternatives to nuclear establishments which are located predominantly in rural areas of high unemployment. In the present political and economic climate it seems hardly feasible to imagine a trade union leader being dispatched to somewhere like Trawsfynydd or Thurso to persuade nuclear personnel that they should relinquish their jobs for the sake of 'the environment'.

The politics of protest and the intense monitoring of nuclear establishments and of other proven and potential sources of environmental pollution (like acid rain) must continue. But it should be paralleled by major efforts on all sides to overcome the poverty of imagination and information which apparently imprisons us within the confines of this dilemma.

Our inability to envisage employment alternatives in these areas can be explained partly (though by no means wholly) by the scandalously secretive nature of the way in which information relating to a civil process – the nuclear generation of electricity – is handled. The Environmental Select Committee, for example, accused the nuclear industry of 'defensive secretiveness' about its work. This attitude, it was alleged, had served only to heighten public anxiety and to engender within the industry a sense of frustration which has led to a virtual 'paralysis' in the key area of radioactive waste management.[5] This 'paralysis' has infected virtually the whole public consciousness. We have accepted for far too long the convenient assumption that the business of nuclear generation and waste disposal is somehow naturally the preserve of an elite whose relationships with the spheres of public accountability and political control are at best ill defined and at worst downright dishonest and potentially disastrous.

The CEGB's weary practice of holding up its hands in gestures of innocence at charges of being one of the EEC's main acid rain polluters is but another facet of this bankrupt obstinacy. Its absurd coyness and reticence when confronting its accusers on this issue reflects a general unwillingness among British industrial managers, politicians and many trade union leaders to confront what is essentially an economic dilemma. No one denies with any degree of seriousness the charge that power station effluent is playing a major role in fouling the physical environment. Yet the deliberate hedging continues on the task of implementing available measures to reduce the size of the problem.

A mining constituency MP with considerable experience in these matters informed me recently that, in his view, anyone involved either in the coal-mining or generating industry who 'harps-on' about acid rain is 'nothing less than a traitor'. The member in question is not a philistine, nor is he unique. He is someone who senses that, if the acid rain boat is rocked too violently, it will result in the capsize of public faith in the virtues of coal-burn and a consequent shift of favour toward increased nuclear generation. Conversely, there are dangers also in the possibility that the CEGB and the government's various atomic agencies will suddenly throw open a small door in their steel wall and start throwing money at the public in an attempt to circumvent vexing planning procedures and to solve their problems *à la France*. Indeed, the enormous nuclear programme in the Republic has generated even more serious difficulties of waste disposal than those faced in the UK. The French appear to have handled the situation both with greater technical and organizational sophistication and, more worryingly, with an audaciousness which will no doubt appeal to the more arrogant amongst our home-grown nuclear mandarins.

ANDRA, the waste management subsidiary of the Commissariat à l'énergie Atomique (CEA) has identified a site near the village of Soulaines, 130 miles east of Paris, which it considers ideal for the storage of low-level nuclear waste. To overcome what little local resistance it met either in the area or nationally, ANDRA set about providing as much information as possible to the local population and local councillors on the characteristics of a low-level waste deposit. More appositely, the French government is offering a £2.74 billion lump sum plus an annual income of £137 million to the commune or communes in which the deposit will be placed. As the European Energy Report commented, 'For a dying village like Soulaines, with only 250 inhabitants, the "nuclear dustbin" could be a salvation.'[6]

It remains to be seen whether the French anti-nuclear groups can muster sufficient resistance to prevent Soulaines from succumbing to this overwhelming financial temptation, but there is no doubt that both the CEGB and the UK government's atomic energy agencies will have noted this tactic with great interest. Little or no discussion has taken place within the labour movement, however, about how it might be possible to confront such a move were it to be attempted in this country. As so often in the past, the most likely scenario will be one in which an unholy alliance of greens, local opponents, concerned trade unionists, politicians and public will find itself casting frantically around for an effective countermeasure to yet another government initiative.

Clearly, it would be infinitely more desirable for those concerned about environmental matters to be in a position to formulate and present their own initiatives. At the moment, however, there seems little chance of firm initiatives being agreed even within the trade union movement, let alone throughout the whole constellation of 'concerned' bodies. There is little chance, for example, that the left's much-vaunted aim of creating an 'integrated energy policy' will become a reality in the forseeable future; firstly, because no one can decide just what kind of 'mix' is acceptable to all of the unions involved and, secondly, because the prevailing political ethos is one of encouraging a fragmentation of energy supply in the name of 'free competition'.

The privatization of large areas of oil and gas production and distribution will be followed by further moves to deregulate and 'denationalize' lucrative sectors of the electricity and coal industries. All of these moves will, in turn, tend to compound the present difficulties associated with monitoring the health, safety and 'environmental' consequences of these operations.

Ironically, this may provide the most promising opportunity for the construction of a kind of new unity. No single group or organization can carry out the monumental task of convincing the public (and their own members) of the overriding importance of protecting themselves and their environment from further physical deterioration or pollution. Recognizing that fact, we have few choices remaining other than to climb out of our trenches and begin discussing seriously the exchange of information and experience which might allow us to mount long-overdue campaigns to secure a future for our people, our industries, our resources and our environment.

8. New Priorities for Environmental Campaigning

Joe Weston

Campaigning politics

The style of campaigning adopted by any particular group or organization largely depends upon its ultimate aims. As pedestrian a point as this may seem, its understanding is crucial for the development of our new approach to environmental politics. For prior to any discussion of campaigning priorities we must be aware of both the possibilities and limitations of campaigning; we must also know more of our own capabilities and shortcomings, and we must be aware of the 'system' in which we are to operate.

As stated in Chapter 1, the single-issue, community pressure group tends to be fairly radical in its approach and style of campaigning. With a clear campaign goal – to protect or enhance their local environment – its members shed their inhibitions and display an apparent readiness to go straight for the political jugular. Local people, raising local issues important to their local community, are much better equipped to display this radicalism than are the larger national bodies. The issues they take up have an immediacy and urgency not present in most national campaigns and there is no real need to attract widespread support and thus dilute their demands. They have, therefore, a freedom experienced by few other political actors.

With the larger, national environmental groups, campaigns tend to have many facets and often incorporate a 'trade off' between an absolutist position and a more pragmatic acceptance of what their campaigns can realistically achieve. Because of this, they tend to address specific identifiable issues which are popular enough to attract funding. These also tend to be issues which are realistically achievable: which means the campaign goal has to be obtainable within the limitations of the political and economic status quo. Furthermore, their campaigns need to lend themselves to visible political activity – like radioactive waste but, apparently, unlike freedom of information. This cocktail of campaign requirements has tended to mean that success is measured in newspaper column inches rather than in real political or social change. Indeed the role of the media is of fundamental importance to all pressure group activity, with campaign strategies being orientated towards the maximum 'cover'.

For political parties, campaigns are very different. With the whole purpose of a political party being electoral victory and the gaining of political power, campaigning success is measured by votes gained, rather than by any actual changes in government policy. The campaigns of the political party are therefore organized around the persuasion of people to switch political allegiance and not around the achievement of specific goals. After all if, for example, the Labour Party actually won a campaign – that is, persuaded a Tory government to change a particular policy – it would lose one of the sticks with which it beats the government. In fact it would enhance the government's standing by illustrating how reasonable it is. This would then mean that Labour would have less ammunition with which to fight the next election. The party of opposition cannot afford to win victories on issues because these serve only the interests of the government, whereas the party of government campaigns for little more than a limitation of the damage caused by the campaigns of its opponents.

In order to win votes from others, a party has to attract the support of people who had previously supported other parties. It therefore adopts policies and campaigns which will be attractive to them – its erstwhile opponents – and hence to the majority of the electorate, which consequently produces policies that do not threaten the status quo. This type of continuous electoral competition tends to erode the differences between opposing parties; it acts as an ideological leveller, reducing all to an appeal to the lowest political common denominator.

Over the past few years we have seen this in action, as the Labour Party has attempted to win back the votes it lost in 1979 and 1983. In place of the radical policies of a reforming socialist party, Labour has increasingly fallen in step with the emerging new political consensus. The policies which could actually have done something about poverty and environmental decay have been replaced by a return to the quasi-corporatist policies which failed the working class throughout the 1960s and 1970s.[1] Furthermore, to prove to the watchful SDP supporter – whom Labour needs to win over – that the party can be trusted with government, they held a witch-hunt of the Liverpool far left in 1985–6.

Given electoral politics, this is a quite understandable and legitimate strategy for the Labour Party to adopt. Without electoral success Labour would die, and to gain that success it has to be pragmatic and single-minded. It has to accept Neil Kinnock's view that

There must be no activity in this Labour movement that is superior to the purpose of winning – of defeating our enemy.[2]

'Winning', in the political climate of the 1980s, means persuading the 'soft' Tories to vote Labour; which inevitably means Labour must once again become a 'soft' Tory Party. Policies which attempt to make fundamental changes to the environment, address the root cause of poverty and tackle problems like street violence in a sensitive, progressive manner will never win over the 'soft' Tories to Labour, for they would, by necessity, erode the wealth and power of the middle-class voter. So the Labour Party, despite its left wing, is drawn ever closer to the new 'enterprise culture' political consensus.

Electoral politics have always tended to disenfranchize minorities in this way: policies which win the votes of the many are often at the expense of the few. As the majority of people in Britain are still comparatively wealthy, it will be that wealth and its maintenance which will dictate the programmes of all the political parties. High levels of unemployment and city-centre rioting will be contained, rather than remedied, and poor, black and disabled people will remain marginalized because they lack the power, wealth and political clout to shape their environment or their lives. It is a situation which even the greens' cure-all, proportional representation, will do nothing to reverse.

It is here, among the disenfranchized, that campaigning social environmentalism has its future. Free of the constraints of party affiliation, campaigning groups could become the champions of those left in the shadows by capitalist market economics and electoral politics. By establishing radical community campaign groups – local people tackling local problems – we can begin to take up the most fundamental of contemporary environmental issues. What is more, by tackling real issues in the same innovative and imaginative way as has been employed to protect wildlife, this new environmentalism could begin to change the whole political climate in Britain. After all, only by moving public opinion back to the left will it be possible for a Labour government to implement radical socialist policies. As was the case in 1945 and 1979, radical policies can be implemented only when the mass of the electorate support those policies. It is no good expecting a Labour government, elected by 'soft' Tories, to carry out radical social change. We must, as greens have long argued, build support for such change from the bottom up. We can do this through campaigning political action which attempts to win victories on issues rather than simply win votes. By making the lives of ordinary people less alienated and by bringing improvements to their physical and social environment, we can win that support and thus begin to re-create the kind of socialist consensus which existed just after the Second World War. And yet, in our attempt to do this, we must remain completely aware of the difficulties and problems with which we will be faced.

Facing reality

In the first five chapters of this book we looked at the way in which the capitalist system shapes both the environment and the people who inhabit it. From such evidence it would be easy to fall into complete despair. After all, we are faced with an economic juggernaut which seems impervious to the political pebbles we hurl at it. The sheer unorganized, chaotic global might of capitalism is a protection against attack as it gives the whole system an air of 'naturalness' an appearance which is reinforced by the illusion of individual freedom, used by its supporters as an ideological weapon against the divided forces of change. This dominance over our lives makes the classical Marxist denouncement of political action seem very attractive as it provides us with an explanation for our failures and a justification for doing nothing. Indeed, as we survey the history of political action, we can see how futile have been the attempts to drag some control back from capitalist economics. Almost a century after the creation of the British Labour Party we are governed by a party which has successfully steered the country into an acceptance of the 'realities' of international market forces; a party which despite mass unemployment still enjoys the support of a significant number of working-class people. After decades of socialist and liberal enlightenment the social divisions are greater, poverty is more entrenched and environmental degradation just as acute.

Yet before we fall into a feeling of complete hopelessness we should survey the successes – though they be minor in comparison – and the ideas which, with more widespread support, could have made a difference. Economic interests have, on occasions, been defeated; political action has brought social changes which have improved the lives of millions of ordinary people. It was political action which widened the franchise in Britain to include women, eroded institutionalized racism in the USA and has made 'nature' such an important issue over the past few years. So despite the obvious hegmonic power that wealth and social class provides, other social interests and demands can sometimes prevail.[3]

Political action is therefore important and can bring some – at least incremental – changes. It may offer only a limited potential, but political action remains all we have. After all, the accumulated power and wealth held by the transnational corporations (TNCs), and the influence they have over all the nations of the world, may well make a nonsense of the pluralist theory of politics; but that power also makes a nonsense of the revolutionary dreams of Marxism. Whether we like it or not, the Soviet Union and China have clearly demonstrated that the creation of 'true' socialism, in single countries, is all but impossible: the tentacles of capitalist economics are long and embrace all, no matter where we live or what social system we live under.[4] And as capitalism appears to thrive on 'crisis' we can't even hope for a spontaneous collapse. The very concept 'crisis of capitalism', so widely used by the left in the early 1980s, is a highly optimistic interpretation of what has happened to capitalism over the past few decades. The massive profits of the TNCs, and their continued growth, make this notion appear completely ridiculous. If anything, what has occurred is more a crisis for labour than for capitalism. The relocation of manufacturing in the Third World has brought more and more labour into the capitalist productive process, creating the ideal conditions for international capital as workers the world over are forced to compete with each other for jobs.[5]

So, despite all its limitations, we are left with politics as the only means through which we can pursue social change. This we must accept and use to our best advantage. We must build a campaigning politics which attempts to win attainable goals; attempts to improve the lives of ordinary people today, rather than attempting to build a socialist or ecological utopia for the future. A politics which understands the limitations and possibilities which exist under capitalism, which recognizes that campaigning on social environmental issues is far more difficult than campaigning for the protection of butterflies and bunny rabbits – a fact which is already painfully obvious to those currently involved in such campaign work. Saving hedgerows does not confront capitalism in the same way as do issues related to poverty; poverty is, after all, of crucial importance to capitalism and has to be maintained in order to preserve the balance of power in market relationships.[6] Furthermore, unlike wildlife protection, social environmental issues confront capitalism head on; they cannot be accommodated within the system for they call for a complete reversal in the way we make use of and distribute resources.

Nevertheless, through a socialist critical theory approach – an approach which is critical of the present without drawing up utopian 'blueprints' for the future – it will be possible to identify the campaign areas which social environmentalism can take on. From the kind of research and analysis already being carried out by socialist and green writers, we can produce campaign priorities which can galvanize people into action and begin to address the issues which are the most relevant to ordinary people. In creating the conditions in which we can begin to build a new political climate in Britain, we can pave the way for a new era when the 'enterprise culture' is replaced by a culture of caring.

Issues and ideas for social environmentalism

In September 1985 the centre of Birmingham was shaken by scenes of obscene violence, as mostly black youths repeated the inner-city rioting which had occurred in Britain for the first time only four years earlier. Shocked and dismayed by the new levels of violence displayed in Handsworth, social scientists and politicians began making conflicting claims as to the cause of the riot. Some blamed unemployment and poverty, while others simply repeated the same complacent, often racist, arguments which have dominated discussions on Britain's inner-city problems.

The weeks and indeed the days preceding the Handsworth riot had seen massive political concern for the inequality, oppression and poverty of black people. Yet this had not been a concern for the people of Handsworth, Toxteth, Brixton or Southall, where such problems have been endemic. No, the television news stories and the newspapers had been dominated that summer by events in Africa – the starvation in Ethiopia and the new wave of troubles in South Africa.

For those already suffering the full weight of the Tory government's economic policies, this concern for Africa – however justified that concern might be – must have seemed like further evidence of the long-standing neglect of black peoples' problems at home. To justify this neglect by arguing that British blacks are not starving and do have the vote is to ignore the very real problems they experience. When you are poor, faced with institutionalized discrimination and racism and have no means of dragging yourself up from the despair created by unemployment, it must seem like a very fine distinction between an African shanty town and a British inner city. And it is a distinction which is being eroded daily by the forces of international capitalism as it places more and more people into competition with each other for jobs and resources. And what clearer evidence is there that the Third World exists here in Britain than when the people of wealthy Surrey send food aid to the poor of Middlesbrough?[7] As we saw in Chapter 5, this erosion of the geographical definition of the Third World is being experienced every day, in real terms, by the people of Britain's inner cities, as they are forced into impoverishment by the same forces which are acting against the poor all over the globe. It is this, the environment of the marginalized and the deprived, which is both the biggest challenge and greatest priority for social environmentalism. Moreover, in Britain it is the environment of the inner city where all who claim to have a concern for either the environment or social justice should most concentrate their efforts.

At present it would appear that all the major political parties see the solution to inner-city problems in financial terms alone. For the Tories it is simply a question of taking control out of the hands of locally elected councils and handing the inner cities over to private capital for development. For most others it is a matter of providing money for 'infrastructure investment'. Yet throwing money at problems is only half the answer. As Home Secretary Douglas Hurd pointed out, 'This government has poured £20 million into Handsworth alone in the past few years':[8] he might have added 'with little effect', for that money has achieved very little. Money is obviously of use only if it is spent effectively; that is, on creating the conditions in which real social change can take place. The inner-city partnership schemes and the Urban Aid Programme have spent money, and lots of it, yet it has been spent on containment, on cosmetic tinkering, rather than on change. Indeed the very structure of these schemes mitigates against their having anything other than cosmetic effect. They are controlled by the Department of the Environment – hence, since 1979, by the Tory government – which has a veto over the way the local authorities, which receive these special grants, spend their money. With most inner-city local authorities being controlled by in many ways highly progressive

Labour councils, the initiatives which have been proposed have tended to be in ideological opposition to the Tory government's overall economic strategy. This has meant that the use of grant money for tackling the root cause of the inner-city problems has been vetoed, while only the cosmetic schemes get approved. Hence we find the gaily painted bridges of London's Hackney, while the social fabric of the area is crumbling.[9]

There are further problems in the way even these largely irrelevant schemes are implemented. In a capitalist state, such as Britain, it is the economic criterion of capitalism which is used to determine how public money is spent, which invariably means that it must produce an economic return rather than a social effect. A consequence of this is the putting out to tender the work of inner-city environmental improvements. As a result that work tends to be carried out by contractors who are based outside the area where the work is to be done while the local unemployed stand by watching. This type of insensitive and unhelpful use of public money is also found in the implementation of the Youth Training Scheme. Rather than giving local people the money to carry out community projects, we find young people being bussed in from outside, doing jobs which older people, with families to support, could have done and benefited from. No wonder such work is so often vandalized soon after completion, for having been rejected by international capitalism and dumped by their own government the young unemployed of the inner cities are not even trusted with the job of improving their own environment. Having been told, in countless ways, that local facilites do not belong to them and are not their responsibility, is it any wonder that people are so willing to further the decay of their environment by vandalism?

If that £20 million which Douglas Hurd spoke of had been spent in Handsworth, at the direction of Handsworth people, making use of local skills and local labour, those who live there may have been a little less willing to burn the place down. For not only would such use of public money have placed wages into the pockets of local people, and thus stimulated the economy of the whole community, but people tend to be less likely to destroy what they themselves have created. They are much more likely to have a pride in their neighbourhood and a greater sense of community if they have been made responsible for their environment and been given the resources that enable them to carry out that responsibility. Imposing an environment, whether through charity or the market, will never encourage a sense of belonging to a community, something which is crucial if people are to stand up and defend their local environment.

So, if policies are implemented more sensitively and with less emphasis placed upon economic criteria and more upon creating social change, there is scope, even within the present system, to improve the environment of the inner city. However, we cannot rely on a Tory, Alliance or even, in the near future, a Labour government to promote this type of departure from accepted uses of public money. For the government, of whichever party, will insist upon its control of public spending and will therefore continue to suffer from the problems which all 'outsiders' face in addressing the problems of particular communities.

I am white and live in a village, and despite my working-class background cannot pretend to understand the needs of those who are black and live in inner-city areas (apart, that is, from understanding the obvious need to end the poverty and racism which they experience). Each community has its own problems, needs and priorities, which only local people can truly identify. For that reason all communities need to win some measure of control over their lives and over the way resources are spent locally. For that to become possible there needs to be a fundamental change in the administration of public money and the organization of local politics in Britain. To bring about that change campaigning political action is necessary from both national and local environmental organizations in alliance with the whole labour and trade union movements. Part of that action would need to include action by community groups, demonstrating the needs and problems of their own communities through the same kind of imaginative and enthusiastic action with which the green movement save hedgerows. Outside of the party political system, local and national groups should campaign together on this issue; for both red and green futures depend upon achieving the kinds of changes which will provide local people with more control over the environment in which they live.

So a major priority for both reds and greens is the campaign to win, for communities, greater control over their local environment. This can begin with the promotion of a new approach to the spending of public money. We hear a great deal from the Alliance, Labour and from greens of the need to spend more money on infrastructure – housing, road maintenance, sewers, and so on – as a means of creating employment and improving the environment. As vital as these programmes obviously are, we need to change the whole structure of public expenditure before they can be implemented. It would be little more than a further fuelling of capitalism, and hence a maintaining of poverty and inequality, to give all this work to the TNCs now eagerly awaiting such an opportunity. Social environmentalists should be campaigning *now* to ensure that the capital expenditure programmes, which seem certain to follow Thatcher's demise, are orientated towards the needs of people in their communities rather than for the benefit of international capital. All this work must be carried out by local authorities, employing local people who have a say in where and how this money is to be spent.

Furthermore, national and regional land use planning tends to mean planning for capitalism rather than for people. The national 'need', for a new road or power station, really means the 'need' for the state to provide the facilities through which capitalism can increase profits and operate more effectively. Too often in the past this has meant an assault upon the environment of ordinary people, with the poor always losing when it comes to the 'fight' over the location of environmentally damaging projects. To change this will require a complete reversal of the present land-use planning system, with local neighbourhoods having far greater influence than is presently the case. Although, as the present division of the country into rich south and poor north clearly demonstrates, there will always be a need for national and regional planning to ensure that people can enjoy equal opportunities wherever they live, this could still be structured around the concept of local control of the environment.

Such a profound change will, however, be resisted with the full weight of both the state and the TNCs, as the present structure is at the heart of the modern capitalist system; the full implementation of decentralized planning will probably remain a utopian dream. Yet this is not to say that such changes should not be campaigned for. Even if never fully implemented, demands of this type can bring some incremental changes which will be of benefit to people and their environment.

Even the act of campaigning can in itself bring changes, both in people and in the whole political climate. One such change could be the re-creation of the sense of community which has been in such decline in recent years.[10] Working together, struggling to bring improvements to the environment of the neighourhood, produces a unity which is diametrically opposed to the individualism fostered by capitalism. It appeals to a sense of co-operation and solidarity which is essentially both red and green, for it produces a recognition of common problems and needs while building a loyalty to the whole community which transcends the individual's desire to rise above the crowd.

Yet we must, as we have throughout this book, emphasize the difficulties. Community solidarity rarely springs up spontaneously – especially in working-class communities – for the pressures of modern capitalism continuously drives people away from each other and inwards upon their own individual problems. Yet there have already been some innovative moves towards creating conditions under which communities can be rebuilt. There have, for example, been the neighbourhood offices set up by some of the more progressive Labour councils. These offices, in places like Walsall and Hackney,[11] have shifted attention away from the faceless bureaucracy of the Social Service's offices to a local office where officers know and understand the problems of the community they serve.

More imaginative still have been the self-help community projects launched by a number of Friends of the Earth local groups. Coventry Friends of the Earth, for example, set up an 'Eco-Street' in the late 1970s, which transformed the whole character of an old and dilapidated street within the inner city. The idea behind the scheme was to involve all the residents of a single street in a fund-raising venture, the proceeds of which were to be used to finance improvements to the street. 'Eco-Street' collected newspapers which were sold for recycling, and the proceeds were used to insulate the homes of the residents. Apart from the obvious savings in heating fuel costs this provided, there were also some very interesting and promising side effects. The project brought together people who, in some cases, had not spoken to each other for many years. People met and discussed their problems and decided together on the best use of the money they had raised. Soon they began to come together on other things too; solving each other's problems, skill swapping and generally helping each other as individuals who were part of a united community. Brought together around a single project, the street became the community it had been a generation or so before. Today, although a key individual involved in setting up the scheme has moved away, the street's new-found spirit remains intact.

Without minimizing the difficulties either of getting such schemes underway, or of ensuring the provision of a council neighbourhood officer, such initiatives can provide the basis upon which a new sense of community can be built. With neighbourhood officers seeking out the individual most likely to become a catalyst for such projects, providing the resources and administrative back-up, it would be possible to create radical campaigning communities which will win back at least some measure of control over their lives.

Yet even without the facility of a neighbourhood officer – or until their widespread introduction – we, as individuals living in communities, should all take on the responsibility and challenge of tackling local environmental problems. This could mean, for example, mounting a campaign against the use of your street as a short-cut for cars and lorries. The people of Hayfield Road in Oxford did this, and through their campaign have created a community spirit which will be difficult to destroy.[12] But in each community the issues which galvanize people into action will be different. For some it will be the fundamental problems like housing; for others it may well be 'green issues' like pollution or the protection of a local amenity. Wherever you live there is no shortage of issues which need addressing, only a shortage of people willing to take them up.

Often, behind this unwillingness to 'get involved' is the belief that there is nothing that an individual or small group can achieve. This belief is a major ally of capitalism for it helps to perpetuate the notion that the system is somehow 'natural', that there is 'no alternative'. The electoral success of Thatcher is clear evidence of the widespread view that we should accept the 'realities' of the market and not fight back. And how often have campaigners been faced with the argument that 'progress' – whatever its consequences – cannot be resisted and that once a government has made up its mind to do something nothing can be done to change it? It is this kind of thinking which we are going to have to destroy, and only radical community campaigning can do it.

The smallest political act can help to break down the feeling of helplessness and apathy which keeps people from challenging the system under which they live. I know of a woman who had become depressed and frustrated by the bad condition of the road outside her home. Every time she went out she had to struggle with her child's pram through ruts, pot-holes and puddles, making her already overburdened life even more difficult to cope with. Feeling it not 'her place' to complain, and not even sure who to complain to anyway, she did nothing but let the state of the road fuel her depression. Then she met some members of a local Friends of the Earth group who provided her with one of their 'pot-hole cards' – a postcard which points out to the local highway authority that if the sender suffers any damage as a result of the reported road condition then the council will be sued for damages. She filled it in and within a few weeks the street had been repaired. That success transformed her whole outlook; suddenly she had found that she could make a difference; she could do something about improving her environment and her life. She has since taken a leading role in many other local campaigns – with mixed levels of success.

Campaigning success is seldom that easy or change that dramatic, yet participation can help to erode the apathy and despair which keeps so many people silent. The experience of the peace and green movements illustrates the way in which political action is important in its own right: taking part in a campaign, sharing ideas and burdens, can often be as beneficial and uplifting as a victory. What is more, political action always politicizes those taking part. The more our communities confront the causes of their problems the more we will recognize and appreciate the problems of others until, eventually, we realize that we are all linked to an international economic order which has made victims of ordinary people everywhere. From this realization we will begin to understand that our community is just a member of a worldwide network of local communities, all of which share similar problems. This produces a world view which is in complete contrast to the nationalist competitive view of capitalism; for it is a view which recognizes the community of the oppressed and impoverished throughout the globe.

It is this wider sense of community – built upon local political action – which will finally erode the differences which people now see between each other. By identifying the common cause of our problems we will slowly end the racism and sexism which the capitalist labour market has imposed upon us. Furthermore, it will be through the creation of radical campaigning community groups that we will begin to bring about real change in the Third World. As so many writers, including Michael Redclift, have already shown, the problems of Africa, South America and Asia are rooted here in the west, in our consumer patterns and the created 'needs' of capitalism. By building social environmentalism, from the bottom up, these 'needs' can be replaced and the people of other nations freed from the yoke of our consumerism. This is not to say that we should allow the poor of the Third World to continue suffering until we reshape our own society – far from it. Of course we should continue to provide aid and at the same time form alliances with campaigning groups within the Third World, but we need to change people's attitudes here if we are to achieve any measure of change for the poor elsewhere in the world. And the best way to change attitudes is not through education and 'creating a new consciousness'. The best way is through political action which frees people from their own poverty and oppression sufficiently to enable them to look at the problems of people elsewhere.

This total community approach to environmental problems will inevitably be slow to build and difficult to maintain. Often it will mean that people with specific skills will have to take up the problems of people in other communities. Indeed, the people presently involved in 'green campaigns' should now begin to take up the issues of the social environment, using their skill to illustrate what can be achieved. People living in the most run-down areas will not necessarily know how to make use of the media, produce campaign material or have the necessary administrative skills to run a campaign, so it is important that those people with such skills make them available to those whose environment is in most need of change. Obviously there are dangers here. It would be so easy for 'outsiders' to take up issues which are wholly irrelevant to local people – the green movement already suffers from a certain degree of middle-class elitism which tends to miss the real needs of others. Furthermore, groups may already be operating within a community which will feel threatened by the formation of a new radical group. To minimize these problems alliances need to be formed between greens, trade unionists and local people to identify the most important issue in a particular community. Once this is established all the 'outsider' efforts should be concentrated upon the creation of a community group which is independent of all national organizations, has a democratic structure and has access to people with campaigning skills and a knowledge of fund-raising. Once a group is well established the 'outsiders' should be able to drop out and either go on to establish new groups elsewhere or return to the issues of their own community.

The issues which should be taken up are those which cause the greatest frustration and anger among local people rather than those which on the surface look to be the most important. This will often require a very fundamental reassessment of the campaigners' own priorities, for it is pointless attempting to build radical community action around issues which local people have little interest in. It may also mean that campaigners find themselves taking up issues which, in comparison with their present work, seem depressingly unglamorous. There can never be the same sense of urgency in campaigning to have a pavement resurfaced as there is in compaigning to save a rainforest. Yet it is issues like poor housing, bad road surfaces, violence, vandalism, speeding vehicles, pavement parking and a lack of facilities for young adults and children which cause the most frustration within communities and upon which local campaigns will have to be built.

Campaigning futures

What we have attempted to do in this book is look at the areas of human experience which best illustrate the need to redefine the way we understand and campaign for the environment. Those areas – the Third World, the urban environment, peace and technology – also highlight the fallacy of the pluralist notion that we live in a meritocratic 'industrial society'. Furthermore they provide us with a whole new set of campaigning priorities. Some of these priorities can be tackled by the campaigning community groups I have advocated in this chapter; others require action at both local and national level by an alliance of all those groups and individuals who really do want to see fundamental changes in British society.

As we saw from Kim Howells's chapter, there are massive opportunities for job creation which are both environmentally and socially beneficial. Apart from the field of energy, these possibilities exist in 'waste' recycling and infrastructure investment, areas which can provide real and meaningful work for thousands, eroding the poverty and despair of unemployment. Yet, as Frank Webster and Keith Lambe have shown us, we still have to come to terms with the technological changes which are undermining our ability to determine the kind of employment futures we would like to see. We have to address this real problem and recognize that to win back some control over our future we must gain at least some measure of control over the TNCs which operate either within or from this country. And as David Pepper argued, only a strong, determined, courageous socialist government which enjoys the support of the mass of ordinary people will be able to do this. This can only be achieved by building that support from the bottom up, creating a new awareness of the need to take on the might of the TNCs so that the lives of people here and throughout the world can be improved.

I believe that our best hope in the struggle to build support for radical socialist policies is through the universal introduction into Britain of neighbourhood offices. These offices should be staffed and funded by local authorities yet controlled by a locally elected neighbourhood co-ordinator. Given some local planning powers and provided with adequate resources to carry out a wide range of local community projects, the neighbourhood officer could become the new focal point for all local political activity, thus shifting the political balance towards communities and away from centralized bureaucratic power.

Once established this system could make possible many of the other priorities identified here. Yet until that happens there remain many problems which still need to be urgently addressed. One of these is the pervasive violence which few are willing to address in any meaningful or progressive way. For the right the problem is one of 'law and order'; for the left the violent are victims of the system and need to be protected from the aggressive actions of the police. Both views are over-simplistic and fail to come to terms with the problems which people faced with violence have to endure. The violence we have to deal with is not just the sporadic inner-city rioting sparked off by insensitive policing; it includes the violence of robbery, verbal abuse, sexual harassment, vandalism and just plain thuggery. It is violence which, as Jeremy Seabrook has shown us, often condemns many to the prison of their own homes, locked behind barred and bolted doors, too frightened to venture out for fear of the mugger or the rapist. Even if their physical surroundings are quite pleasant, the environmental quality of a community is largely irrelevant if its people are frightened to leave their homes. When I was a child I could leave home early on a summer's morning and play all day long a mile or so from home in Bernwood Forest. Few parents, even in the countryside, allow their children that freedom today, robbing children, for their own good, of the opportunity fully to experience their environment. Because of the ever-present threat of violence we deny our children some of the most important influences upon their development, like the unsupervised companionship of other children, where imagination can be developed free of the constraints of adult 'rules' and values. These threats of violence may have been disproportionately magnified by the media, hungry for the most sensational stories, but, as Mark Levene has argued here, the fear of violence has become part of our social fabric and as such is a massive environmental issue which remains ignored by those who like to call themselves environmentalists.

We have not attempted to produce here detailed answers to the problems we have identified. Our task has simply been one of showing that without a closer alliance between reds and greens such answers will never be found. We have, we hope, shown that such an allegiance is not only possible but crucial if we are going to achieve any significant impact upon the increasing power of international capital and its control over our future. For reds the problem with the community-based environmental approach is one of coming to terms with the need to reject the old-style centrist policies of the Labour Party. For greens it is one of accepting the need to redefine the way we understand the term 'the environment'.

In both cases these changes are beginning to take place. We have already mentioned the decentralization policies of some Labour councils and the creation of the neighbourhood offices: a major move away from the traditonal 'we know best' approach of state socialism and a move towards the 'bottom up' approach of the greens. As for the greens, the movement here is coming from an organization which has long held a real potential for the development of social environmentalism. With its democratic structure and network of local community campaign groups, Friends of the Earth remains one of the best hopes for the future of environmentalism in British. Over the past few years FoE have been increasingly taking up the very issues with which this book has been concerned. In their critique of the Tory government's public transport policies, in their attack upon the horrific slaughter on our roads, in their practical recycling projects which are creating jobs up and down the country, and in their energy policy which challenges the profit motive behind electricity generation, Friends of the Earth are clearly already social environmentalists. This fact is further displayed when they argue the case for their tropical rainforest campaign. Gone are the political ecology arguments of overpopulation and the conservation arguments for absolute protection. What FoE campaign for is the sustainable use of the forests by people for people. While acknowledging from the very beginning,

> such a campaign will inevitably engage us in a wide-ranging analysis of the problems, the root of which is the desperate poverty of many TRF nations.[13]

Here is recognition, then, from one of Britain's most influential environmental organizations, that behind arguably the world's most pressing ecological problem is poverty. It is a social issue and not an ecological one at all.

Notes and References

The place of publication of books and articles is London, unless otherwise stated

Introduction

1 Bahro, R., *Building the Green Movement*, GMP, 1986, p. 13.
2 Fleischman, P., 'Conservation, The Biological Fallacy' in *Landscape* 18, 1969, pp. 23–7.
3 Seabrook, J., *Landscapes of Poverty*, Basil Blackwell, Oxford, 1985, p. 151.
4 The Environment Minister, William Waldegrave, became the Tory government's 'green Minister' in 1985, having special responsibility for the 'green' environment. See *Observer*, 12 January 1986.
5 Bahro, R., *The Alternative in Eastern Europe*, New Left Books, 1977, p. 262.
6 Worsley, P., *The Three Worlds*, Weidenfeld & Nicolson, 1984.
7 Harrison, P., *Inside the Inner City*, Penguin, 1985.
8 Springsteen, B., *Born in the USA*, CBS (86304), 1984.
9 Bruce Springsteen, Wembley Stadium, 6 July 1985.

Chapter 1

1 Patterson, W., 'A Decade of Friendship: The First Ten Years' in Wilson, D., *The Environmental Crisis*, Heinemann, 1984, p. 140.
2 Cowley, J., *Housing, for People or for Profit?* Stage I Books, 1979, p. 8.
3 See Burgess, R., 'The Concept of Nature in Geography and Marxism' in *Antipode* I0 (2), 1978, pp. 1–11; also Pepper, D., *The Roots of Modern Environmentalism*, Croom Helm, 1984, Chapter 6.
4 Redclift, M., *Development and the Environmental Crisis*, Methuen, 1984, pp. 45–6.
5 Pepper, D., *The Roots of Modern Environmentalism*, Chapter 7.
6 Lowe, P. and Goyder, J., *Environmental Groups in Politics*, Allen & Unwin, 1983, p. 25.
7 Worsley, P., *The Three Worlds*, Weidenfeld & Nicolson, 1984, p. 337.
8 Ehrlich, P., *The Population Bomb*, Pan/Ballantine, 1968; Hardin, G., 'The Tragedy of the Commons' in *Science* 162, 1968, pp. 1243–8. For a more detailed discussion of these and the other influential works of the

period, see: Pepper, D., *The Roots of Modern Environmentalism*, Chapter 1, and Sandbach, F., *Environment. Ideology and Policy*, Basil Blackwell, Oxford, 1980.

9 Blowers, A., *Something in the Air*, Harper & Row, 1984, p. 216.

10 Cotgrove, S., *Catastrophe or Cornucopia*, John Wiley & Sons, 1982, p. 5.

11 Ehrlich, P. and Harriman, R., *How To Be A Survivor*, Ballantine Books, 1971, p. 11.

12 See Pepper, D., *The Roots of Modern Environmentalism*, Chapter 4.

13 *The Ecologist, A Blueprint for Survival*, Penguin, 1972.

14 *ibid.*, p. 15.

15 Edward Goldsmith has been one of the most influential of writers in the development of green politics. He co-wrote *A Blueprint . . .*, is editor of *The Ecologist* and has also written *The Stable Society*, The Wadebridge Press, Wadebridge, 1978.

16 Ecology Party, *Politics for Life*, The Ecology Party, 1983, p. 4.

17 Although it should be stated that the Friends of the Earth Transport Campaign is now addressing this issue. See Chapter 8.

18 For detailed discussions on pluralist ideas and concepts, see Gamble, A., *An Introduction to Modern Social and Political Thought*, Methuen, 1981, Chapter 6; Giddens, A., *The Class Structure of the Advanced Societies* (2nd ed), Hutchinson, 1981; Kumar, K., *Prophecy and Progress*, Penguin, 1981, Chapter 6.

19 See Bell, D., *The End of Ideology*, Collier, New York, 1961; Bell, D., *The Coming of the Post-Industrial Society*, Basic Books, New York, 1973; Bell, D., *Sociological Journeys*, Heinemann, 1980; Dahrendorf, R., *Class and Class Conflict in Industrial Society* (1959), Routledge & Kegan Paul, 1976; Galbraith, J.K., *The New Industrial State*, Penguin, 1969.

20 Ecology Party 'Towards a Green Future: Extracts from the Common Manifesto of the European Green Parties' in *Econews*, Ecology Party, June 1984, p. 1.

21 Porritt, J., *Seeing Green*, Basil Blackwell, Oxford, 1984, p. 49.

22 See 19 above.

23 Galbraith, J.K., *The New Industrial State*, p. 396.

24 See Ecology Party, *Politics for Life*.

25 See Goldsmith, E., *The Stable Society*; Porritt, *Seeing Green*; also, Ash, M., *Green Politics: The New Paradigm*, The Green Alliance, 1980.

26 Bell, D., *The Coming of the Post-Industrial Society*.

27 Capra, F., *The Turning Point*, Fontana, 1983.

28 See Leland, S., 'Feminism and Ecology: Theoretical Connections', in Caldecott, L. and Leland, S. (eds), *Reclaim the Earth*, The Women's Press, 1983, pp. 46–58; also, Capra, F., 'The Ying, Yang Balance', in *Resurgence* 86, 1981, pp. 12–15.

29 Capra, F., *The Turning Point*, p. 462.

30 Porritt, J., *Seeing Green*, p. 117.

31 See Pepper, D., *The Roots of Modern Environmentalism*, Chapter 7.

32 See Williams, R., *Socialism and Ecology*, Socialist Environmental and

Resources Association, 1982.

33 See Hill, C., *The World Turned Upside Down*, Temple Smith, 1972, and Hill, C. (ed.), *Winstanley: The Law of Freedom and Other Writings*, Pelican, 1973.

34 Sandbach, F., *Environment. Ideology and Policy*, p. 202.

35 Kitchen, G., *Development and Underdevelopment in Historical Perspective*, Methuen, 1982.

36 In particular, Schumacher, E.F., *Small is Beautiful*, Harper & Row, 1973.

37 Hardy, D., *Alternative Communities*, Longman, 1979, p. 25.

38 See Porritt, J., *Seeing Green*, Chapter 7 and Ash, M., *Green Politics: The New Paradigm*.

39 See Kraushaar, O., 'America: Symbol of a Fresh Start' in Moment, G. and Kraushaar, O. (eds), *Utopias; The American Experience*, Methuen, 1980; also Pollack, N., *Populist Responses to Industrial America*, Norton Library, New York, 1966.

40 See Worsley, P., *The Three Worlds*, p. 43.

41 Capra, F. and Spretnak, C., *Green Politics: The Global Promise*, Hutchinson, 1984, p. xix.

42 Kitchen, G., *Development and Underdevelopment*, p. 30.

43 Cotgrove, S. and Duff, A., 'Environmentalism, Middle Class Radicalism and Politics' in *Sociological Review* 28, 1980, pp. 333–49.

44 Gouldner, A., *The Future of Intellectuals and the Rise of the New Class*, Macmillan, 1979.

45 Cotgrove, S. and Duff, A. in *Sociological Review*, p. 341.

46 *ibid*.

47 'Teachers: Not Working', the *Economist*, 27 September 1985, pp. 31–2; also Flather, D., 'The Sack of Academe' in *New Statesman* 110 (2846), pp. 10–12.

48 See Massey, D., 'The Shape of Things to Come' in *Marxism Today*, April 1983, pp. 18–27; Massey, D. and Meegan, R., 'The New Geography of Jobs' in *New Society*, 17 March 1983, pp. 416–17; also Seabrook, J., *Landscapes of Poverty*, Basil Blackwell, Oxford, 1985, Chapters 1 and 2.

49 Seabrook, J., *ibid*.

50 Bellini, J., *Rule Britannia*, Abacus, 1982, Chapter 3.

51 Ecology Party, *Politics for Life*, pp. 9–11.

52 Douglas, M., *Purity and Danger*, Penguin, 1970; Douglas, M., 'Environments at Risk' in Benthall, J. (ed.), *Ecology, the Shaping Enquiry*, Longman, 1972, pp. 129–45.

53 Worsley, P., *The Three Worlds*, p. 337.

54 See Dale, R., 'Nation State and International System: The World-System Perspective' in McLennan, G. *et al* (eds), *The Idea of the Modern State*, Open University Press, Milton Keynes, 1984, pp. 183–207; Frobel, F. *et al*, *The New International Division of Labour*, Cambridge University Press, Cambridge, 1980; Redclift, M., *Develop-*

ment and the Environmental Crisis, Chapter 1; Worsley, P., *The Three Worlds*, Chapter 5.

Chapter 2

1 See *Guardian*, 11 July 1983.
2 Porritt, J., *Seeing Green*, Basil Blackwell, Oxford, 1984, p. 161.
3 Eqbal Ahmed, 'The Peace Movement and the Third World' in *END Journal*, April/May 1985.
4 Requoted in *Bombs for Breakfast*, Committee on Poverty and the Arms Trade, 1981, p. 8.
5 Glazier, D. and Dibblin, J., *Pacific Region, Background of the Arms Race*, END (unpublished) 1985.
6 Exposed in 'Britain's Other Islanders', *World in Action*, Granada TV, 21 June 1982.
7 Barnett, R.J., *The Lean Years*, Sphere Books, New York, 1980, p. 229.
8 Pinckerley Harrison, J., *The Endless War*, Macmillan, New York, 1982, p. 256.
9 'No Victor in the Gulf', *The Times* (editorial) 23 September 1985; 'Killing for Arms Dealers', *Observer*, 5 August 1984.
10 Campbell, D., articles on US war plans for the UK in *New Statesman*, 6 and 13 September 1985.
11 *Guardian*, 24 January 1983; *Daily Mail*, 9 November 1983.
12 Chafer, T., 'Politics and the Perception of Risk, A Study of the Anti-Nuclear Movements in Britain and France' in *West European Politics*, 8, I, January 1985, pp. 5–23.
13 Quoted in 'Hooligan', Thames TV, 20 August 1985.
14 Seabrook, J., 'The Seeds of Violence', *Guardian*, 3 June 1985.
15 See 'Non-Nuclear Defence' in The Ecology Party, *Peace, A Green Broadsheet*, 1985, pp. 8–9, and Porritt, *Seeing Green*, p. 156.
16 Tatchell, P., *Democratic Defence, A Non-Nuclear Alternative*, GMP Books, 1985.
17 Seabrook, J., *Guardian*, 3 June 1985.
18 See *Embrace the Earth*, CND Publications, 1983, pp. 30–1.
19 Shwarz, W., 'The Missiles of Misery', *Guardian*, 23 December 1983; Mushausen, J.M., 'The Cycle of Peace Protest in West Germany' in *West European Politics*, 8, I, January 1985, pp. 24–40.
20 'Women Form a Web', *Oxford Star*, 10 October 1985.
21 The title of a chapter in Raymond Williams's *Towards 2000*, Chatto & Windus, 1983.

Chapter 3

1 On the use of the charge of 'nostalgia' to defeat criticism of 'progress', see Lasch, C., 'The Politics of Nostalgia: Losing History in the Mists of Ideology' in *Harper's*, 269 (1614), November 1984, pp. 65–70.

2 See Newby, H., *Green and Pleasant Land? Social Change in Rural England*, Hutchinson, 1979.
3 Martin, J., *The Wired Society*, Prentice Hall, Eaglewood Cliffs, New Jersey, 1978, p. 4. This is also an American phenomenon; see Marx, L., *The Machine in the Garden: Technology and the Pastoral Ideal in America*, Oxford University Press, New York, 1964.
4 Toffler, A., *The Third Wave*, Collins, 1980, p. 135.
5 Toffler, A., *Future Shock*, Bodley Head, 1970, p. 284.
6 Toffler, A., *The Third Wave*, p. 167.
7 Toffler, A., *Future Shock*, p. 233.
8 Toffler, A., *The Third Wave*, p. 367.
9 *ibid.*, p. 247.
10 *ibid.*, p. 294.
11 *ibid.*, p. 375.
12 Martin, J., *The Wired Society*, p. 191.
13 Toffler, A., *Future Shock*, pp. 282–3.
14 cf. Hall, S., 'The Culture Gap' in *Marxism Today*, January 1984, pp. 18–22.
15 Marx, K. in Marx, K. and Engels, F., *Collected Works*, Vol. 38, Lawrence & Wishart, 1982, p. 99.
16 cf. Webster, F., 'The Politics of New Technology' in Miliband, R. and Saville, J. (eds), *Socialist Register 1985*, Merlin, 1986, pp. 385–413.
17 See Robins, K. and Webster, F., 'New Technology: A survey of trade union response in Britain' in *Industrial Relations Journal*, 13, I, 1982, pp. 7–22.
18 *Microelectronics: A Labour Party Discussion Document*, 1980, pp. 22, 38.
19 See Bailes, K.E., *Technology and Society under Lenin and Stalin*, Princeton University Press, Princeton, 1978.
20 Marx, K. and Engels, F., *Manifesto of the Communist Party* (1848), Foreign Language Press, Peking, 1936, p. 36. They continue:

   The bourgeoisie, during its rule of scarce one hundred years, has created more massive and more colossal productive forces than all preceding generations together. Subjection of Nature's forces to man, machinery, application of chemistry to industry and agriculture, steam-navigation, railways, electric telegraphs, clearing of whole continents for cultivation, canalization of rivers, whole populations conjured out of the ground – what earlier century had even a presentiment that such productive forces slumbered in the lap of social labour? (p. 37)

21 See Webster, F. and Robins, K., *Information Technology: A Luddite Analysis*, Ablex Rublishing Corp., Norwood, New Jersey, 1986, Chapter 4.
22 cf. Robins, K. and Webster, F., 'Luddism: New Technology and the Critique of Political Economy' in Levidow, L. and Young, B. (eds), *Science, Technology and the Labour Process*, Vol. 2, Free Association

Books, 1985, pp. 9–48.

23 David Owen, *Marxism Today*, March 1983, p. 28.

24 Evans, C., *The Mighty Micro: The Impact of the Computer Revolution*, Gollancz, 1979, p. 208.; Hyman, A., *The Coming of the Chip*, New England Library, 1980, pp. 126–7.

25 On socialist conceptions of post-industrialism see Gorz, A., *Farewell to the Working Class: An Essay on Post-Industrial Socialism*, Pluto Press, 1982; Gorz, A., *Paths to Paradise: On the Liberation from Work*, Pluto Press, 1985 (Gorz's review of Toffler, pp. 81–91, is especially revealing of commonalities between socialists and futurists); Block, F. and Hirschhorn, L., 'New Productive Forces and the Contradictions of Contemporary Capitalism: A Post-Industrial Perspective' in *Theory and Society*, 5, 1979, pp. 363–95.

26 See the important essay by Noble, D.F., 'Present Tense Technology' Parts 1–3 in *Democracy* 4, 1983, pp. 8–24, 70–82, 71–93.

27 Callaghan, J., *Prime Minister Announces Major Programme of Support for Micro-electronics*, Press Notice, 10 Downing Street, 6 December 1978.

28 *Hansard*, 11 July 1980, col. 933–4.

29 *ibid.*, col. 938.

30 *ibid.*, col. 1000.

31 Williams, S., *A Job To Live: The Impact of Tomorrow's Technology on Work and Society*, Penguin, 1985, p. 52.

32 Patrick Jenkin, when Minister of Trade and Industry, coined this phrase, but it is applicable to all three main political parties.

33 See Braun, E. and McDonald, S., *Revolution in Miniature: The History and Impact of Semiconductor Electronics*, Cambridge University Press, Cambridge, 1978, especially Chapters 6–9.

34 See Noble, D.F., *Forces of Production: A Social History of Industrial Automation*, Knopf, New York, 1984; Wilkinson, B., *The Shopfloor Politics of New Technology*, Heinemann, 1983; Shiken, H., *Work Transformed: Automation and Labour in the Computer Age*, Holt, Rinehart & Winston, New York, 1985.

35 *Annual Report*, Thorn-EMI, 1980.

36 Quoted in Wainwright, H. and Elliott, D., *The Lucas Plan: A New Trade Unionism in the Making?*, Allison & Busby, 1982, pp. 114–15.

37 On IBM, see Malik, R., *And Tomorrow . . . The World?*, Millington, 1975; Sobel, I., *IBM: Colossus in Transition*, Times Books, 1981.

38 See Webster, F. and Robins, K., *Information Technology: A Luddite Analysis*, Chapter 7.

39 Dodsworth, T. and Taylor, P., 'GM Takes a $5 Billion Gamble', *Financial Times*, 6 June 1985.

40 *Structural Issues in Global Communications*, The Tobin Foundation, Washington DC, 1982, p. 25.

41 'International Information Flow: A Plan for Action' in *Business Roundtable*, New York, January 1985, pp. 6, 10–11. Cited in Schiller, H.I., *National Sovereignty and the World Business System*, paper

presented to the International Political Science Association XIII World Congress, Paris, 19 July 1985 (mimeo).

42 Gooding, K., 'Ford's 'Do It Only Once' approach' in *Financial Times*, 16 November 1984.

43 cf. Murray, F., 'The Decentralization of Production – The Decline of the Mass-Collective Worker?' in *Capital and Class* 19, Spring 1983, pp. 74–99.

44 Quoted by Hall, D., 'AT&T To Make Telephones in Singapore' in *Financial Times*, 8 July 1985.

45 See Schiller, H.I., 'Breaking the West's Media Monopoly' in *The Nation*, 21 September 1985 pp. 248–51; Nordenstreng, K., *The Mass Media Declaration of UNESCO*, Ablex, Norwood, New Jersey, 1984.

46 Eckelmann, R., 'A Study of the International Competitive Position of the US Telecommuications Equipment Industry' in 'High Technology Industries: Profiles and Outlooks', *The Telecommunications Industry*, US Department of Commerce, International Trade Administration, April 1983, US Government Printing Office, Washington DC, 1983, Table 11, p. 18.

47 'Network Move Blocked' in *Computer News*, 16 May 1985.

48 Eckelmann, R. in *The Telecommunications Industry*, p. 13; cf. Schiller, 'The Storming of the PTTs' in *Datamation*, May 1983, pp. 155–8.

49 de Jonquieres, G., 'Crossed Lines in an $80bn Industry' in *Financial Times*, 5 July 1985.

50 Bracken, P., *The Command and Control of Nuclear Forces*, Yale University Press, New York, 1983. On the frailty and vulnerability of C3I systems, see Ford, D., *The Button: The Nuclear Trigger – Does it Work*, Allen & Unwin, 1985.

51 See Barnaby, F., 'Microelectronics in War' in Friedrichs, G. and Schaff, A. (eds), *Microelectronics and Society: For Better or For Worse*, Pergamon Press, Oxford, 1982, pp. 243–72; Hoag, P.W., *High-Tech Armaments, Space Militarization, and the Third World*, British Sociological Association Annual Conference, Hull, 1985 (mimeo); Jasani, B., *Outer Space – A New Dimension of the Arms Race*, Taylor & Francis, 1982.

52 Quoted in Marsh, P., 'Blast-off for Star Wars Research Programme' in *Financial Times*, 16 May 1985.

53 Tucker, A., 'Who Really Needs Eureka?' in *Guardian*, 1 August 1985. On the way in which military burdens hinder British and US capital's efforts to escape recession, see Kaldor, M., *The Baroque Arsenal*, Hill & Wang, New York, 1981; Maddock, Sir I., *Civil Exploitation of Defence Technology*, Report to the Electronics Economic Development Committee, National Economic Development Office, February 1983.

54 'The SDI, Eureka and Industry', *Financial Times* Conference, 4 and 5 November 1985, Skinner's Hall, London. Speakers included Lord Chalfont (ex-Labour Minister, now director of IBM UK); Dr G.A. Keyworth (Science Advisor to the President and Director, Office of

Science and Technology Policy); M. Clark (Deputy Chairman, Plessey); Dr G. Yonas (Chief Scientist, SDI Organization); H. Metcalfe (Deputy Managing Director, British Aerospace); M. Jean-Louis Gergorin (Senior Vice-President, Matra); Dr A.E. Puckett (Chairman, Hughes Aircraft Company).

55 McCrone, J., 'Alvey Shows a Defence Bias' in *Computing*, 5 September 1985, p. 14.

56 Bracken, P. (*see* note 50) ponders: 'One must ask if democratic government could survive a nuclear war because of the need to violate grossly the constitution in some attack situations, combined with the shock to democratic institutions of the resulting exchange (p. 200). Jungk, R., *The Nuclear State*, Calder, 1979, argues that nuclear energy/power undermine liberties because they presume a permanent crisis of security. cf. Sagan, S.D., 'Nuclear Alerts and Crisis Management' in *International Security* 9, 1985, pp. 99–139.

57 Campbell, D., 'Secret Laws for Wartime Britain' in *New Statesman*, 6 September 1985, pp. 8–10; Campbell, D. and Forbes, P.,' If War Came Close We Would Have New Masters' in *New Statesman*, 13 September 1985, pp. 10–11.

58 Burnham, D., *The Rise of the Computer State*, Weidenfeld & Nicolson, 1983, p. 121. Burnham also notes that for the last three decades 'the NSA probably was the single largest source of federal research dollars spent in the development of advanced computers and thus was a significant but silent force in the shape of an industry that reaches into every aspect of American life' (p. 122); cf. Bamford, J., *The Puzzle Palace: America's National Security Agency and its Special Relationship with Britain*, Sidgwick & Jackson, 1983; Powers, T., 'The Ears of America' in *New York Review of Books* XXX, I, 3 February 1983, pp. 12–14.

59 Davies, N. and Black, I., 'Subversion and the State' in *Guardian*, 17 April 1984, p. 19; cf. Leigh, D., *The Frontiers of Secrecy: Closed Government in Britain*, Junction Books, 1980, Chapter 5.

60 Davies, N. and Black, I., 'Techniques in Eavesdropping on the Public' in *Guardian*, 18 April 1984, p. 6.

61 Leigh, D. and Lashmar, P., 'Revealed How MI5 Vets BBC Staff' and 'The Blacklist in Room 105' in *Observer*, 18 August 1985, pp. 1, 9.

62 See Bookchin, M., *Towards an Ecological Society*, Black Rose Books, Montreal, 1980, p. 129; cf. Ignatieff, M., *The Needs of Strangers*, Chatto & Windus, 1984, p. 52; Seabrook, J., *Landscapes of Poverty*, Basil Blackwell, Oxford, 1985.

63 Schiller, H.I., *Who Knows: Information in the Age of the Fortune 500*, Ablex, Norwood, New Jersey, 1981, p. 136.

64 Sahlins, M., *Stone Age Economics* (1972), Tavistock, 1974, p. 3.

65 See Ewen, S., *Captains of Consciousness: Advertising and the Social Roots of the Consumer Culture*, McGraw-Hill, New York, 1976; Pope, D., *The Making of Modern Advertising*, Basic Books, New York, 1983.

66 See Schudson, M., *Advertising, The Uneasy Persuasion*, Basic Books, New York, 1984, Chapters I and 5.

67 See Galbraith, J.K., *The Affluent Society* (1958) Penguin, 1968.

68 This is elaborated in Webster, F. and Robins, K., *Information Technology: A Luddite Analysis*, Part Three.

69 See Robins, K. and Webster, F., 'Information, Television and Social Taylorism' in Drummond, P. and Peterson, R. (eds), *Television in Transition*, British Film Institute, 1985.

70 cf. de Certeau, M., 'On the Oppositional Practices of Everyday Life' in *Social Text* 3, 1980, pp. 3–43.

71 In spite of our general indebtedness to ecological principles, as regards IT, we note a tendency amongst some greens to welcome this technology with little reserve (see Porritt, J., *Seeing Green*, and Ecology Party, *Politics for Life*). We would resist this, contending that the principles that greens apply to nuclear power and agriculture should also apply to computer communications technologies.

Chapter 4

1 Brown, F. *et al.*, *State of the World*, W.W. Norton & Co., 1984.

2 Global 2000 *Report to the President*, Penguin, 1982.

3 *World Conservation Strategy: UK, The Conservation and Development Programme for the United Kingdom*, Kogan Page, 1983, p. 321.

4 Sanchez de Carmona, L., 'Ecological Studies for Regional Planning in the Valley of Mexico' in di Castri, F., Baker, F. and Hadley, M. (eds), *Ecology in Practice*, UNESCO, 1984.

5 Diaz, B., *The Conquest of New Spain*, Penguin, 1963.

6 Morales, H.L., 'Chinampas and Integrated Farms: Learning from Rural Traditional Experience' in di Castri *et al.*, *Ecology in Practice*; also Toledo, V.M. *et al.*, 'Critica de la ecologia politica' in *Nexos* 47, Mexico, 1981.

7 Wittfogel, K., *Oriental Despotism*, Random House, New York, 1981.

8 Fores Cano, E., *Origen y Desarrollo de los Problemas Agrarios de Mexico (1500–1821)*, Ed. Era, Mexico, 1981.

9 Gibson, C., *Los Aztecas Bajo el Dominio Espanol*, Ed. Siglo XXI, Mexico, 1981, pp. 312, 362–4.

10 PRUSDA, *Comision Coordinadora Para el Desarrolla Agropecuario del Distrito Federal*, Mexico, 1984.

11 Farvar, M.T., 'Interaction of Social and Ecological Systems' in Mathews, W. (ed.), *Outer Limits and Human Needs: Resource and Environmental Issues of Development Strategies*, Dag Hammarskjold Foundation, Uppsala, 1976.

12 *World Conservation Strategy, UK*.

13 *ibid.*, p. 333.

14 *ibid.*, p. 335.

15 Rosenbaum, W., *The Politics of Environmental Concern*, Praeger, New

York, 1973, p. 252.

16 Farvar, M.T. and Glaeser, B., *Politics in Ecodevelopment – A Cart Before the Horse?*, Science Centre, Berlin, 1979.

17 Buttel, F. *et al.*, 'Biotechnology in the World Agricultural System' in *Cornell Rural Sociology Bulletin* 144, 1985.

18 Norgaard, R., 'Coevolutionary Agricultural Development' in *Economic Development and Cultural Change* 32, 3, 1984.

19 Ewell, P. and Poleman, T., *Uxpanapa: Agricultural Development in the Mexican Tropics*, Pergamon Press, Oxford, 1980.

20 IBRD, *Environment and Development*, The World Bank, Washington DC, 1979.

21 Redclift, M.R., 'Mexico's Green Movement' in *The Ecologist* (in press).

22 Source, Toledo, A., *Como Destruir el Paraiso*, Centre de Ecodesarrollo, Mexico City, 1985.

23 Blaikie, P., *The Political Economy of Soil Erosion in Developing Countries*, Longman, 1984.

24 Norgaard, R., 'Traditional Agricultural Knowledge: Past Performance, Future Prospects and Institutional Implications' in *American Journal of Agricultural Economics* 66, 5, 1984, pp. 874–8.

25 McNeely, J. and Pitt, D. (eds), *Culture and Conservation: the Human Dimension in Environmental Planning*, Croom Helm, 1984.

Chapter 6

1 Porritt, J., *Seeing Green*, Basil Blackwell, Oxford 1984, p. 118.

2 Morrissey, J., 'Red and Green Health' in *Fourth World Review*, 1984, pp. 11–14.

3 Ecology Party, *Politics for life*, The Ecology Party, 1983.

4 Porritt, J., *Seeing Green*.

5 Capra, F., *The Turning Point*, Wildwood House, 1982.

6 Pender, P., 'Reds and Greens in Europe' in *New Ground* 6, 10 and 15, 1985.

7 Bookchin, M., *Towards an Ecological Society*, Black Rose Books, Montreal, 1980.

8 See Lowe, P. and Worboys, M., 'Ecology and the End of Ideology' in *Antipode* 10, 2, pp. 12–21.

9 Porritt, J., *Seeing Green*, p. 165.

10 Pender, P. in *New Ground*.

11 Schumacher, E.F., *Small is Beautiful*, 1973, and *Good Work*, Abacus, 1980.

12 *New Ground* 4, 1984, p. 2.

13 Anderson, V., 'What Is New Economics?' in *New Ground* 6, 1985, p. 9.

14 Elkins, P., 'Conventional Economics is Bunk' in *Green Line* 37, 1985, pp. 3–4.

15 Pepper, D., *The Roots of Modern Environmentalism*, Croom Helm, 1984.

16 Ward, C., 'Housing and Real Socialism' in *New Ground* 7, 1985, p. 5.

17 Kropotkin, P., *Fields, Factories and Workshops (Tomorrow)* (1899), ed. Colin Ward, Unwin, 1974.

18 *The Ecologist, Blueprint for Survival* in *The Ecologist* 2, 1, 1972, pp. 1–43.

19 Callenbach, E., *Ecotopia*, Pluto Press, 1978, and *Ecotopia Emerging*, Banyan Tree Books, Berkeley, California, 1980.

20 Newby, H., *Green and Pleasant Land* (new edition), Wildwood House, 1985, Chapter 6.

21 *Outline Prospectus For a Third Garden City*, Town and Country Planning Association, 1979.

22 *Greentown: Proposal for the Development of the Crowhill Site, Milton Keynes*, The Greentown Group, 1981, and Page, A., 'The Dartlington Model of the Community for the Future' in *Future Communities*, Institute of Contemporary Arts, 1981.

23 For more details of these, see Pepper, D., *The Roots of Modern Environmentalism*; Hardy, D., *Alternative Communities in Nineteenth-Century England*, Longman, 1979; Campbell, A., Keen, C., Norman, G. and Oakeshott, R., *Worker-Owners: The Mondragon Achievement*, Anglo-German Foundation for the Study of Industrial Society, 1977.

24 For convincing analyses of the middle-class nature of most environmentalism in Britain, see Cotgrove, S., *Catastrophe and Cornucopia*, John Wiley, 1983; Sandbach, F., *Environment, Ideology and Policy*, Basil Blackwell, Oxford, 1980.

25 Wilson, D., 'No Simple Answer', *FoE Supporters Newspaper*, Autumn, 1985.

26 White, L., 'The Historic Roots of Our Ecological Crisis' in *Science* 155, pp. 1203–7.

27 See Pepper, D., 'Determinism, Idealism and the Politics of Environmentalism' in *International Journal of Environmental Studies* 26, pp. 11–19.

28 Cspel, A., 'Marxism and the Ecological Crisis' in *East European Reporter*, source, SERA 1985.

29 Cook, R., 'Towards an Alternative Ecological Strategy' in *New Ground* 2, 1984, pp. 11–14.

30 Kinnock, N., 'Turning Over a New Leaf' in *New Ground* 5, 1985, pp. 4–5.

31 Secrett, C., in Blunden, J. and Curry, N., *The Changing Countryside*, Croom Helm, 1985, p. 215.

32 Carver, J., 'Comrades or Clients?' in *New Ground* 3, 1984, pp. 9–10.

33 Cook, R. in *New Ground* 2.

34 *New Ground* 5, 1985, p. 3 (Editorial).

35 *Financial Times*, 7 February 1985.

36 Harvey, D., *Limits to Capital*, Basil Blackwell, Oxford, 1982.

37 Wagstaffe, H. and Emerson, T., 'Wanted – A Real Strategy For Jobs' in *New Ground* 3, 1984, pp. 15–16.

38 Ward, C., 'Housing and Real Socialism' in *New Ground* 7, 1985, p. 5.

39 *New Ground* 3, 1984, p. 3 (Editorial).
40 *Greenpeace News*, August 1985, Letter p. 4.
41 Carver, J., 'Comrades or Clients?' in *New Ground* 3, 1984, pp. 9–10.
42 O'Brian, J., 'Labour-Eco Alliance' in *New Ground* 6, 1985, p. 3.
43 *Guardian*, 4 October 1985.
44 Elliot, D., 'SERA and the Trade Unions' in *New Ground* 7, 1985, pp. 8–9.
45 Jacobs, M., 'Bhopal Update' in *New Ground* 7, 1985, p. 16.
46 Kitching, G., *Rethinking Socialism*, Methuen, 1983, p. 5.
47 Roberts, A., 'Roles for Labour' in *New Ground* 4, 1984, p. 9.
48 Kinnock, N. in *New Ground* 3.

Chapter 7

1 Hertsgaard, M., *World View 1985*, Pluto Press, 1984, p. 4.
2 *ibid.*
3 Sweet, C., 'A View of the Future: A Return to Energy Policy', unpublished paper presented to the conference The Future of the Electricity Supply Industry, Polytechnic of the South Bank, London, June 1985.
4 Holmes, A. and Parrott, M., *Financial Times Energy Economist* 47, September 1985, p. 5.
5 See Brown, C., 'MPs Fail to Agree on Nuclear Waste Report', *Guardian*, 17 December 1985, p. 2.
6 *Financial Times European Energy Report*, 200, 18 October 1985, p. 8.

Chapter 8

1 See Benett, A., 'The Void Kinnock Can't Fill', *Guardian*, 30 December 1985, p. 6.
2 Quoted in Raphael, A. *et al.*, 'Neil Kinnock – "Leader at Last" ', *Observer*, 6 October 1985, p. 11.
3 See Hall, S., 'The State in Question' in McLennan, G. *et al* (eds), *The Idea of the Modern State*, Open University Press, Milton Keynes, 1984, p. 26.
4 See Brucan, S., 'The State and the World System' in *International Social Science Journal* XXXII, 4, 1980; Frobel, F. *et al.*, *The New International Division of Labour*, Cambridge University Press, Cambridge, 1980; Radice, H. (ed.), *International Firms and Modern Imperialism*, Penguin, 1975; Tugendhat, C. *The Multinationals* (1971), Penguin, 1984.
5 *ibid.*
6 See Seabrook, J., *Landscapes of Poverty*, Basil Blackwell, Oxford, 1985.
7 Reported on 'London Plus', BBC I TV, 18 December 1985.
8 Interviewed on 'The Jimmy Young Show', BBC Radio 2, 11 September 1985.

9 See Dean M., 'Accounting for the Cities of Inner Despair', *Guardian*, 3 October, 1985, p. 21; Cunningham, J., 'Britain's Shattered Cities are Led Up the Garden Path', *Guardian*, 19 November 1985, p. 21; also Loughlin, M. *et al* (eds), *Half a Century of Municipal Decline*, George Allen & Unwin, 1985; Harrison, P., *Inside the Inner City*, Penguin, 1985.
10 See Seabrook, J., *Landscapes of Poverty*, Chapters 1 and 2.
11 For a description of the neighbourhood offices in operation, see Seabrook, J., *The Idea of Neighbourhood*, Pluto Press, 1984.
12 'Good Neighbours', *Oxford Mail*, 10 September 1985, pp. 14–15.
13 Editorial, *FoE Newspaper*, Summer 1985, p. 2.